"Maid in the Market"

*Women's Paid
Domestic Labour*

edited by
Wenona Giles & Sedef Arat-Koç

**Fernwood Publishing
Halifax**

Editing: Brenda Conroy
Design and production: Beverley Rach
Printed and bound in Canada by Hignell Printing Limited

A publication of
Fernwood Publishing
Box 9409 Station A
Halifax, Nova Scotia
B3K 5S3

Canadian Cataloguing in Publication Data

Main entry under title:

Maid in the market

Includes bibliographical references.
ISBN 1-895686-35-0

1. Women domestics—Canada. 2. Service industries workers—Canada. 3. Sex role—Canada. I. Giles, Wenona Mary, 1949- II. Arat-Koç, Sedef.

HD6072.2.C3M35 1994   331.4'8164046'0971   C94-950080-1

CONTENTS

ABOUT THE AUTHORS

Sedef Arat-Koç, Assistant Professor, Women's Studies, Trent University, Peterborough, Ontario

Jane Bertrand, former President of the Ontario Coalition for Better Childcare, Early Childhood Education Faculty, George Brown College, Toronto, Ontario

Wenona Giles, Assistant Professor, Social Science Department, Atkinson College, Centre for Refugee Studies, York University, North York, Ontario

Audrey Macklin, Assistant Professor, Faculty of Law, Dalhousie University, Halifax, Nova Scotia

Patricia McDermott, Associate Professor, Social Science Department, Faculty of Arts, York University, North York, Ontario

Rusty Neal, Assistant Professor, Maritime School of Social Work, Dalhousie University, Halifax, Nova Scotia

Ester Reiter, Associate Professor, Social Science Department, Atkinson College, York University, North York, Ontario

Mary Romero, Associate Professor, Department of Sociology, University of Oregon, Eugene, Oregon.

ACKNOWLEDGEMENTS

The authors would like to thank the following persons for their insightful critiques, comments and encouragement during the preparation of this book: Bonnie Fox, Meg Luxton, Patricia McDermott, Linda Peake, Ester Reiter.

We are also grateful for the interest and editorial suggestions of Errol Sharpe, the copy editing assistance of Brenda Conroy and the production assistance of Beverley Rach, who together brought this book to press.

INTRODUCTION

Sedef Arat-Koç & Wenona Giles

As "traditional" households composed of the breadwinner husband/ father and the full-time homemaker wife/mother become a minority phenomenon in most advanced industrial countries, the questions of who is going to do housekeeping and caregiving work, and how, remain unresolved. People, women especially, try very hard to juggle public work with domestic responsibilities. Such efforts are almost always individualized (rarely recognized and supported by the community and/or the state) and are seldom successful. In this sense, the present period in most advanced industrial countries can be characterized by a "crisis of the domestic sphere" (Arat-Koç 1989).

Despite this continuing crisis, feminist discourses of the 1980s and the early 1990s, compared to those of the 1960s and the 1970s, have been marked by a relative absence of critical analysis of, and alternatives to, the present forms of reproductive work. This book aims to continue what we consider was an important emphasis, during the earlier part of the second wave of feminism, on reproductive work. Specifically, our focus is women's paid reproductive work in the service sector—cleaning, tidying, feeding, and caring for and serving people.

In this book we demonstrate that, even when done in "public" and for pay, the work of housekeeping and caregiving in capitalist society is problematic. We explore how the work of reproduction is subordinated and devalued in the marketplace when it is done for a wage. The book has two principal goals: first, to identify problems with commercial forms of social reproduction; and second, to discuss developing forms of resistance to the conditions of paid domestic work as it is organized in industrial society.

The book focuses on gender and racial/ethnic dimensions of the industrial solution to the reproduction of labour power, in addition to issues of class and the labour process. Paid housework is usually performed by women, especially working-class women and women of

1

subordinate ethnic and racial groups. As feminists have become more aware of the non-universality of women's experiences, the urgency of this kind of study is better recognized. What is needed is a new feminist analysis and politics of reproductive work that will address the relationship between gender, class, and race/ethnic relations to arrive at an evaluation of alternatives for privatized housekeeping and caregiving work.

Feminist theory since the early 1970s has made valuable contributions to an understanding of unpaid reproductive work (Fox 1980; Luxton 1980; Malos 1980). The domestic labour debate has explored the linkages between the "labour of love" of housework and mothering in the private sphere and the functioning of the market economy. Often emphasized is the unpaid nature and the isolation of housework and childcare.

An issue that has not been tackled is what happens to reproductive work that occurs in the public sphere, in the labour market, when it is done for pay. Although there are a number of feminist studies on different types of predominantly female service work (Chaney and Castro 1989; Cock 1980; Glenn 1986; Kalisch and Kalisch 1982; Murphy 1993; Palmer 1985; Reiter 1991; Rollins 1985; Sanjek and Colen 1990), there has not been any theoretical or comparative work that has attempted to bring an understanding to the forms of subordination that reproductive workers in different occupations share. What are also needed are analyses that will inspire and stimulate envisioning of new socialist feminist alternatives to the organization of reproductive work.

Starting from the premise that in capitalist society reproductive interests are subordinated to the drive for profit, this book aims to provide a critical examination of how the profit motive affects the relations in socialized forms of "housekeeping." As Elson has argued, whereas the main concern of capitalist economics has been the production and reproduction of capital, the main concern of socialist economics so far has had a "productionist bias," concerned with wage workplace relations and not addressing relations between the workplace and households (1988:6). A rethinking of socialism that is informed by feminism, must involve a politics of "commitment to the collective self-determination of 'life itself'" (Luxton and Maroney 1992:8, 32).

Historical Precedents

The issue of reproductive labour has always held an important place in feminist theory and practice. Resisting ideologies of familism that identify women as naturally responsible for paid and unpaid reproductive labour, feminists have posed alternative methods and visions of how this work could be reorganized.

As early as the first half of the nineteenth century, the reorganization of reproductive work was a major concern for a group of feminists influenced by the communitarian socialism of Robert Owen and Charles Fourier. Communitarians criticized the traditional family and marriage as institutions that contributed to isolation and women's oppression. As alternatives to the anti-social family and privatized housework and childcare, they offered elaborate schemes, as well as concrete examples of communal living, which would entail the collectivization of all reproductive work. The communities they inspired had collective kitchens, dining rooms, and nurseries (Hayden 1981; Taylor 1983).

Communitarian socialists differed from Marxian socialists in the significance they attached to the reorganization of domestic work. They criticized capitalism for its effects on human work in general. The ideal communities they envisioned and helped to build gave equal emphasis to household labour and industrial labour (Hayden 1981). Subsequently, in the late nineteenth and early twentieth centuries, Marxist socialist critiques of industrial society focused on the organization of industrial work. While the socialization of domestic work was also part of the socialist visions of Engels and Lenin, it lacked the centrality it held in communitarian visions and practice. By the time the first wide-scale socialist experiment was embarked upon in the Soviet Union, early efforts to reorganize domestic work had been subordinated to some "practical" concerns. This motive limited attempts for socialized childcare in the Soviet Union, and the "liberation" of women came to mean liberation for industrial production, rather than putting an end to women's isolation and enslavement in the home.

While state socialism failed to effectively deal with the organization of reproductive work, a forgotten tradition of feminism in the late nineteenth and early twentieth centuries directly addressed the issue. In the United States, three generations of what Dolores Hayden (1981) has termed "material feminists" not only demanded economic remuneration for women's unpaid domestic labour but also offered elaborate proposals for communes, collective kitchens, cooperative housekeeping schemes, and changes in the architecture of homes. While the theory and practice of these women have been extremely useful in offering alternative visions for organizing domestic labour, they did not deal with gender, class, and race issues. They were not concerned with how the reorganization of domestic labour would affect those who (albeit collectively or as paid workers) would continue to perform those tasks. "Material feminists" expressed their concerns for finding efficient and rational solutions to the "waste," "annoyance," "unreliability," and "laziness" of servants through rigid supervision and factory-like discipline imposed by collective housework schemes. Paid houseworkers were neither agents nor intended beneficiaries in these projects, which seemed to prioritize an extension of the principles of industrialization over concerns for equality (Gilman 1966, 1972; Hayden 1981).

While the issue of domestic labour, as one of the areas of women's oppression, continues to be of central concern to many feminists during the second wave of feminism, the attempts to rethink and experiment with the reorganization of reproductive work hardly matches the creativity of nineteenth and early twentieth century feminism. Its symbolic place as an important piece of work marking the beginning of the second wave of feminism and its influence in shaping how liberal feminists approach the issue of reproductive labour makes Betty Friedan's *Feminine Mystique* worth mentioning. For Friedan, housework can be done by "anyone with a strong enough back" (and "a small enough brain") and it is "peculiarly suited to the capacities of feeble-minded girls" (1963:206, 244). When Friedan defined housework in these terms, she defined "women's liberation" for the white, middle-class housewives she wrote for as getting out of the home. What she did not address with her solution to the problem were questions of who the "feeble-minded girls" doing housework would be in a "liberated" world; what their liberation would entail; and how the gender relations that have historically shaped men's non-involvement in domestic labour would need to change to ensure "women's liberation."

In the 1970s, radical and socialist feminists became interested in solutions to the oppressiveness of privatized housework under capitalism. A highly controversial solution was a demand for wages for housework (Dalla Costa and James 1972; James 1976; Malos 1980). It was thought that by receiving a wage for housework, women would be freed from the unequal sexual division of labour *vis-a-vis* unpaid domestic labour. The slogan "wages for housework" was often misunderstood. According to its leading theoreticians, the demand for money for housework was to be the first step towards refusing to do housework. As an attempt to make housework visible and to demonstrate that it is a site of struggle (Federici 1980:258), this movement made a significant contribution to the domestic labour debate. However, as Landes points out, wages for housework would not alter the relations of production in the household nor change the fact that the housewife already shared in the wage packet of the wage earner (Landes 1980:266).

One of the aims of this book is to encourage a return among feminists to questions about domestic labour. We think that the interest over the analysis of and solutions to domestic labour which preoccupied feminists in the 1960s and the 1970s died rather prematurely. The "domestic labour debate" of this period concentrated on theorizing the relationship of domestic labour to capitalism, often at the expense of losing sight of the gender and power relationships it entailed (Armstrong et al. 1985) and at the expense of neglecting to envision alternatives to privatized domestic labour within a (still) capitalist society. The debate focused on questions such as: whether domestic labour produces "value"; whether and how domestic labour is functional to capital; and whether privatized domestic labour is inevitable under capitalism (Benston 1969; Fox 1980; Malos 1980). While the Marxist-feminist analysis of domestic labour has been very valuable in highlighting and making sense of one of the areas of women's oppression, it has not understood power relations in domestic work beyond what it assumed to be economically determined by capitalism. In terms of its central foci and conceptual framework, the debate did not go beyond what Marxist discourse could offer. As one of the contributors to the debate later stated, the domestic labour debate remained, "in its essentials, an attempt to generate Marxist answers to feminist questions" (Seccombe 1986:190).

Despite its many problems, the "domestic labour debate" provided a space where second-wave feminists in the 1960s and 1970s could ponder domestic labour. Even though the personal is still political in feminist discourse, what the feminism of the 1980s and early 1990s has lacked has been continuing analyses of and creative alternatives to the existing forms of reproductive labour. It is the former gap in recent feminism that this book is intended to address. We do not claim to be starting here the more difficult job of developing new strategies for replacing existing forms of (privatized and paid) reproductive work. We leave this to social movements in which we hope academics will participate.

While sharing the criticisms of the domestic labour debate that it has not provided *feminist* answers to questions on women's oppression, we do not believe it would be adequate to provide *feminist* answers if that implies *solely* a concern with issues of gender expressed in universal terms. This volume also aims to deal with the issue of difference in the experience of reproductive work.

Race, Ethnicity, and Gender

As Glenn (1992) pointed out, there has been an underlying assumption of universality of experience in studies that have addressed the domestic labour debate. Gender analysis has predominated in these studies. The different relationships of women of various ethnic/racial backgrounds or different social classes to unpaid domestic labour have not been explored. This represents a serious omission in the research on domestic labour and one that has limited our understanding of the structure of "housekeeping" work.

A number of studies have addressed the different experiences of women of colour to paid domestic work (Arat-Koç 1990; Cock 1980; Glenn 1986; Rollins 1985; Romero 1982; Silvera 1989). These have been important sources of data and analysis on cultural and historical differences in the working experience of women. Studies of gender and class relations in the households of ethnic/racial minorities and immigrant/ migrant women have provided *some* insights into the organization of unpaid domestic labour (Bloch 1976; Dill 1988; Giles 1992, 1994; Glenn 1985, 1986; Labelle et al. 1987; Meintel et al. 1987; Pessar 1984). However, they do serve to point out that the issues of difference have not been adequately addressed in the theoretical literature on unpaid domestic labour. This failure to address ethnic/racial differences in the debates around unpaid domestic labour has also limited our understanding of paid domestic work.

As Glenn states, regions characterized by dual labour systems[1] provide key sites for the study of concepts of gendered and racialized labour (1992:31-32). Some capitalist societies have provided such sites where ethnic/racial minority women, who are also often migrants or immigrants, provide one type of labour that is devalued as opposed to the more highly valued work of white women.[2] This difference is justified as being due to disparities in training, skill, and education (Glenn 1992:33). If, as Glenn points out, race and gender are socially constructed systems, then they "must arise at specific moments in particular circumstances and change as these circumstances change" (1992:31). We need to begin to understand the historical circumstances behind these socially constructed systems with regards to "household" work.

It is essential now to begin to review and revise the earlier debates around unpaid domestic labour, incorporating an analysis that is actively aware of ethnic/racial and class differences. This can be carried out in light of research, particularly over the last decade, on the racial and ethnic divisions in paid "household" work. These studies will not simply add to the earlier studies on domestic labour, but actually inform them and provide insights into ways of further examining the interconnectedness of ethnicity/race, gender, and class in both paid and unpaid domestic labour.

Unpaid Housework and Paid Reproductive Work: Towards Analysis

There is a fundamental contradiction in capitalist society between the production of people and their needs, on the one hand, and the production of commodities for profit on the other. This contradiction has important implications for a study of paid and unpaid domestic work. While the reproduction of labour power is necessary for capitalism, the value of the work that goes into it goes unacknowledged because capitalism, as Karl Marx said, can only survive as long as reproducing labour power can be made to cost less than what labour power could produce (Marx, 1976). Therefore, the dilemma of capitalism is that while the reproduction of labour power is necessary, the capitalist goal is to create profit and thus keep the costs of reproduction low. It is mainly women who do reproductive work and work in the place that has been described as the "interface of productive and reproductive resources and spaces" (MacKenzie 1988:26). When this type of work is paid for, it is mainly women from working-class and ethnic/racial minority groups who provide the capitalist "solution" to the dilemma of reproduction. They do this through paid housework as well as other types of work in the broader service sector.[3]

One of the differences between unpaid housework and paid housework done in the home is that the latter is not regarded as a "labour of love" that is part of the worker's familial responsibility.[4] As well, paid housework is characterized by a significant social distance, usually involving not only class but also ethnic/racial differences, between the worker and those consuming her services (Cock 1980; Glenn 1986; Rollins 1985). Despite this distance in paid housework, such as that performed by domestic workers and nannies, employer-employee relationships may be personal and paternalistic (Arat-Koç 1990; Palmer 1989, Rollins 1985; Romero, this volume; Sanjek & Colen 1990). In other words, the commoditization of some forms of housework does not necessarily result in a total transformation of the relationship between people to a professional one. These kinds of employer-employee relationships generally leave workers vulnerable to abuse from employers, who can elide the more personal side of the relationship at whim.

In forms of paid reproductive and service work which take place in the public sphere, such as the fast-food industry and office or hotel cleaning, the employers are managers of large corporations and the relationships are impersonal and more fully commoditized than in private homes (Reiter 1991; Sacks 1988; Armstrong et al. 1993). In addition, domestic work done in the expanding sectors of these industries is usually labour intensive. It may be combined with technologically advanced methods of production as in the fast-food industry, as Reiter describes in chapter six, or it may be modelled on old "mass production" social relations (Rustin 1989:58) as Neal describes in chapter four (on office cleaning) and Giles in chapter five (on the hotel and catering industry). In the case of fast-food workers, advanced technology leaves nothing to the worker's discretion and further denies individualism through promotion of "the team concept." On the other hand, when workers themselves develop their own "teams" or collectives, these can act as forms of resistance to the oppressiveness of paid domestic work, as both McDermott in chapter seven (on retail workers) and Giles in chapter five (on chambermaids) describe.

The marketing of the illusion that paid domestic service work is created as a "labour of love" occurs in a number of the industries discussed in this volume and results in a variety of contradictory situations—for example, retail workers who have to unpack and carry heavy loads of goods to their department are expected to wear high heels and ensure that their make-up is perfect; fast-food workers are always expected to wear a smile to indicate their pleasure at serving customers; and hotel workers who "sell the hotel" in advertisements extolling their "concern . . . to transform your room into a haven of tranquillity" are barely paid enough to support themselves and their families.

Paid housekeeping work in the service sector is related to unpaid housework in the home in so far as both forms of work are concerned with cleaning living spaces and providing food. As well, these are jobs which are generally done by women, and in the former case most of these women are members of ethnic/racial minority groups. Neither payment for domestic work nor other ways in which the production of goods and services are being commercialized have led to a valorization of reproductive work. Rather, what we see are complex developments uneven in their effects for different groups in society. The effects of ethnicity/race, class, and gender on paid domestic work in dual labour systems lead to very different consequences for different groups of women. This book provides a context for the discussion of these issues and also aims to shed some light on the question of how relations and inequalities between advanced capitalist and post-colonial regions affect the constitution of workers who fill positions of paid housekeeping work.

Common Ground and Difference

In the remainder of this introduction, we draw out from the various chapters in this book what is common as well as different about women's experiences in paid domestic work. Some of the issues raised in the case studies in this volume concern the organization of work, physical hardships, low pay, and unfavourable working conditions, as well as the forms of resistance and labour militancy expressed by women to their working conditions. We are also interested in the ways that gender, class, race, and regional inequalities constitute the status and conditions of workers doing paid "housework."

One of the main concerns of the contributors to this book is the division between a minority of well-paid workers and the many poor women who have no possibility of mobility or improved working conditions. Economic restructuring has affected the organization of paid housekeeping work, as it has other forms of labour. Globally, labour markets have continued to expand, based in part on the availability of a cheap, mainly female, labour force for multinational corporations. The women who are an important part of the expanding labour markets are immigrant or migrant workers who have moved from rural to urban areas or have left their countries to find wage work in transnational corporations, which include not only factories but also hotels, restaurants, contract cleaning companies, and fast-food outlets.

The literature of the last ten years on women and development (Elson and Pearson 1981; Nash and Fernandez-Kelly 1983; Redclift and Mingione 1985; Waring 1988; Mies et al. 1988; Ward 1990; and others) has provided an important framework for examining the global exchange of labour. Unlike manufacturing work which can, with relative ease, be transported off-shore, paid housekeeping work needs to be performed where the demand exists and cannot be uprooted and moved elsewhere if there is labour unrest and an unstable political climate (Sassen-Koob 1984). The demand for reproductive labour exists wherever there is a demand for labour power. The service work involved in the reproduction of the worker cannot be moved to some other part of the world and isolated from the worker her/himself.

This type of work, therefore, is intertwined with migration and economic restructuring in ways that involve specific kinds of state and employer controls, as well as particular living and working conditions, depending upon the type of work and the country of immigration. Migration is a survival strategy for women, many of whom are the sole or principal wage earners in their households. As Macklin demonstrates in chapter one, in most advanced capitalist countries, women who declare themselves as houseworkers or "domestics" to immigration officials are never accepted as permanent workers or potential citizens. Women who migrate to do paid housework work either as temporary workers or illegally. Those who migrate alone to paid domestic jobs often leave partners and children at home and send back remittances while they survive on extremely limited incomes. Or they may migrate as dependant spouses, thus foregoing any of the amenities such as language and job training programs, provided to the "independent" immigrant. As immigrant women, they are in a tenuous and temporary position, which undermines their capacity to protest against inequalities and exploitation in the workplace. Their families are affected by their status in the workplace, as well as by the disruption caused by migration and the poor and sometimes hazardous living conditions experienced by domestic workers who are migrants.

The contributions to this volume focus on three different kinds of paid "domestic work." First are the different forms of commodified housework mentioned in chapters one and two on domestic workers, chapter three on childcare workers and chapter six on fast-food workers. Second is service work performed in commercial settings which is *like* housework. Chapter four on office cleaners and chapter five on hotel chambermaids provide examples of this kind of paid "domestic work." A third type of "domestic work"—that performed by the hotel workers in chapter five, the fast-food workers in chapter six and the department store sales staff in chapter seven—is service work marketed and sold in familistic terms.

The order of chapters in the book represents a move from private to more public and commercialized forms of paid domestic work. The book opens with studies on women who work as cleaners in the home and in the public sphere. Chapter one, by Audrey Macklin, examines the relationship between Canadian immigration laws and the employment of private domestic workers, and raises questions as to the extent that the state is implicated in the exploitation of domestic workers. Macklin also explores the relationship between the Canadian woman, privileged by "race," citizenship, and class, and the foreign, poor woman of colour she employs to perform domestic work in her home. Mary Romero's insights on Chicana domestic workers in chapter two are particularly useful in elucidating the class and racialized nature of this work. She provides an historical analysis of the way that the commoditization of paid housework has changed to adapt to contemporary family structures in the United States. She discusses how workers today are changing the workplace relationship by resisting personalism and control in their jobs—recognizing that "an affective relationship provides more opportunities for exploitation." Jane Bertrand, in chapter three, deals with subordination of childcare workers in Canada, where provinces vary widely in their treatment and remuneration of these workers. She demonstrates the obstacles to professionalization of childcare workers and suggests some solutions, which include an examination of the historical split between education and childcare, thus raising the issue of definitions and valuing of "skill." Her chapter points to the contradiction between the requirements of quality childcare and the difficulty of meeting these requirements through low paid workers.

In chapter four, Rusty Neal discusses resistance as it relates to subcontracted office cleaners in Toronto. She demonstrates how subcontracting contributes to gender, ethnic/race, and class inequalities in the workplace. The differences in the workplace organization of two cleaning sites is compared and related to possibilities for union organization. In chapter five, Wenona Giles links the ethnic and migrant status of Portuguese women to their position as chambermaids. The work of hotel cleaners is "managed" by several layers of professional overseers. Control, racism, the effects of immigrant status, and resistance are central issues in this chapter.

In chapters six and seven, Ester Reiter and Patricia McDermott examine the retail sales of food and goods. McDermott's chapter pushes the boundaries of definitions of paid housekeeping work. She argues that the retail work that women do in a department store in Southern Ontario is actually a form of paid housework. The work of male retail workers is better paid and does not involve housekeeping. Men in this workforce, while ostensibly described in the same terms as women retail workers, in fact, form part of an elite group of "commission sales" employees, earn more, and experience better working conditions. Glenn's critique (1992:37) of the concept of "comparable worth" refers to the concept of a hierarchy of worth and remarks that the "division between 'skilled' and 'unskilled' jobs is exactly where the racial division typically falls." In the case described by McDermott in chapter seven, it is a gender division that defines the elite group of workers, as opposed to those who engage in the less-valued work that involves domestic labour. Related to this, Romero in chapter two gives an historical overview of domestic work in the United States, discussing how the commercialization of housework and household goods has been linked to the depersonalization and reduction of tasks to "unskilled labour power," rather than "skilled labour services." As their work became defined as unskilled labour, paid domestic workers were subjected to similar forms of control as factory workers.

Reiter's research in chapter six addresses problems with both the production and consumption aspects of the capitalist solution to "getting the meal out of the kitchen." While the socialist and feminist attempts to socialize reproductive work have never become widespread, the attempts of corporations, in certain areas like the fast-food industry, have been "successful," at least in capital's terms, in making profits. In human terms, however, the industry is full of problems. The response of the fast-food industry to the human need for food consumption has been neither very affordable nor healthy for the body or the environment. In terms of production, the fast-food industry has not liberated women from the kitchen but has simply brought them to the kitchens of fast-food restaurants. Reiter shows that it is women and teenagers who form the part-time workforce and who are subordinated in unfavourable working conditions in fast-food outlets. Unlike the domestic workers in chapter two, who struggle against the personalism in employer—employee relationships, the workers in the fast-food industry try to humanize a workplace organized along Fordist principles.

All of the contributions to this volume demonstrate the problems with and resistance to the various forms of paid reproductive work as organized in modern capitalist society. Alternative visions as to how else these types of work can be reorganized need to be informed by the feminist, anti-racist, anti-capitalist, and environmentalist critiques developed here. New visions of collectivities that begin the task of creating workable alternatives to the isolation of much paid domestic work in the home, as well as to the loss of control inherent in such practices as the so-called "team" approach used widely in the fast-food industry, need to be developed. The illusions marketed by multinational hotel chains, describing paid domestic workers as wholly devoted to the client's comfort, while the daily needs of these same workers are barely met, have to be countered. The destabilizing position of immigrant or migrant women who are at one and the same time included and excluded—admitted as workers, but barred from worker protection laws—has to be challenged and changed. It is hoped that this book will not only contribute to a better understanding of the social relations inherent in paid domestic work in a capitalist economy but also to changing those relations.

Notes

1. Glenn refers to a relationship between the emergence of "gendered and racialized labour" (1992:32) and dual labour systems where reproductive labour occurs in a structural hierarchy in the market. More privileged and less privileged workers are segregated by time (e.g. nighttime office cleaning) and space (e.g. restaurant kitchens), so that they do not even have to acknowledge or interact with one another.
2. Our reference to "dual labour systems" is not meant to imply that these are two parallel and disassociated workforces. To the contrary, they are interconnected and interdependent labour systems.
3. See Cohen (1987) for data on women in the service sector in Canada.
4. We must qualify this statement, however, as Sanjek (1990) documents the ambiguity which is involved in the recruitment of child household workers in Ghana who are related through kinship ties to their "employers". This was also typical of many other societies—nineteenth century Canadian farm households, for example (Cohen 1988).

CHAPTER ONE

ON THE INSIDE LOOKING IN: FOREIGN DOMESTIC WORKERS IN CANADA

Audrey Macklin

> Why are [guest workers] admitted? To
> free the citizens from hard and unpleas-
> ant work. Then the state is like a family
> with live-in servants. That is not an
> attractive image, for a family with live-
> in servants is—inevitably, I think—a
> little tyranny. (Walzer 1983:52)

And what then are we to make of the state that admits foreigners for the very purpose of furnishing families with live-in servants? This is the question posed by Canadian immigration and employment practices respecting foreign domestic workers.

The laws and policies of labour-importing states such as Canada provide a critical point of articulation for the global migration patterns of domestic workers, such as those surveyed by Lycklama (1989) and the individual worker—employer dynamics described by Romero in chapter two of this book. Canada's immigration schemes funnel the international flow of workers by establishing criteria for who gets into Canada, for how long, and on what terms. Employment laws determine the eligibility of domestic workers for such basic worker protections as minimum wage, maximum hours, and overtime. The operation of these instruments of Canadian state policy necessarily influence the localized distribution of power between particular workers and employers. Taken as a whole, the dynamic characterizing the experience of domestic workers along each of these dimensions may be understood as a destabilizing phenomenon of simultaneous inclusion and exclusion: The domestic worker is admitted into Canada but barred from political membership, employed in a workplace but often excluded from worker-protection laws, resident in a household but not a part of the family.

The purpose of this chapter is twofold: the first objective is to illuminate the ways in which Canadian immigration policy and employment standards legislation participate in the social construction of live-in domestic workers. Of particular interest is the extent to which the impact of the laws varies along an axis of race/national origin. Also, the Canadian regulatory regime is briefly compared to the American one, which formed the backdrop against which the "Zoë Baird incident"[1] transpired early in 1993.

The second objective is to address and problematize a feminist analysis of the relationship between women who work outside the home (like Zoë Baird) and the women they employ inside the home (like Lillian Cordero).

A point of departure is the recognition that live-in domestic work is qualitatively distinct from other occupations and even from live-out domestic work. Virtually all investigations of the occupation reveal that wherever and whenever domestic work is done on a live-in basis, elements of the master—servant relation persist. Because she resides where she works, the domestic worker's workday is potentially unlimited. Her entitlement to privacy often goes unrecognized or unrespected. Her physical (including sexual) and emotional integrity is unusually vulnerable to abuse. Because she does the sort of work that women traditionally perform for free, the economic and social value of her labour is underestimated and its identity as real work belittled by the "labour of love" mystification (Arat-Koç 1989:58). This translates economically into low wages, delinquent payment of wages, unpaid overtime wages, and so on. Because the household is considered the paradigmatic realm of the "private," the protections normally accorded to employees in the workplace are frequently denied to domestic workers on the grounds that state intervention in the private sphere is inappropriate. The domestic worker is not a member of the nuclear family with whom she lives, a reality that employers have often dealt with by treating domestic workers as socially invisible. At the same time, employers' physical, emotional, and time demands preclude the domestic worker from building or sustaining allegiances outside the household. In racially stratified societies, the invisibility of the servant, the invisibility of people of colour, and the invisibility of women's work converge (Rollins 1985:210). Unlike a day worker, a live-in domestic worker has no reprieve from her ascriptive status or, as Mary Garcia Castro (1989:116) phrases it, no "psychosocial space" she can call her own. She exists as the projection of her employers' definition of her in any situation where employers claim the authority to seize her labour.

These aspects of live-in domestic service emerge to a greater or lesser extent wherever the occupation exists, even within societies and families that formally abjure relations of inequality and subordination. As Jane Turritin (1976:99) cautions, the structural and economic inequality between domestic worker and employer means that the employer

> has a great deal of discretionary power with respect to the way in which they interact. . . . The alleged egalitarian, child-centred, middle-class family, promoting equality between husband, wife and children, should not be thought of as guaranteeing similar egalitarian relationships when it comes to hiring help.

Clearly, immigration and employment laws alone do not create the unequal relations characterizing the employer–domestic worker dynamic. At the same time, these instruments of state policy institutionalize the inferior and excluded status of domestic workers; as such, they also contribute to the reproduction of that status.

The Import of Domestic Workers
Historical Overview (Pre-1981)
A survey of the historical literature on the "servant problem" in Canada reveals that, with few exceptions, demand has always exceeded local supply. Live-in domestic service has always provided the least desirable type of legal employment open to women. Few were attracted to it, and most left it as soon as possible. As a result, foreign-born women have always dominated the occupation because native-born women simply refused to do it for the wages and working conditions offered by prospective employers (Barber 1984; Leslie 1980; Roberts 1979).

Not long after Confederation, the government agreed to lend assistance to employers' and recruitment agencies' quest for servants. Its contribution consisted of promoting domestic work overseas as an attractive option for young, single, British women and of subsidizing the cost of passage to Canada. As the twentieth century progressed, the potential sources for suitable servants expanded to include European women. Despite various efforts however, Canada consistently failed to attract and retain sufficient numbers of women to meet the demand. Because the women entered as immigrants with the liberty to choose their employment, they could not be forced to stay in domestic work, so they did not. Curiously, chronic supply-side shortages never seemed to motivate significant numbers of employers to improve wages and working conditions in a bid to retain women in domestic work. Then, as now, wages for domestic work stubbornly resisted the laws of supply and demand.

15

In the early 1950s, pressure from Canadian employers and British Caribbean governments led to the execution of agreements between Canada, Jamaica, and the Barbados that became known as the Caribbean Domestic Scheme. Under the Scheme, single, healthy women between the ages of eighteen and forty with no dependants and at least an eighth-grade education were admitted to Canada as landed immigrants on condition that they remain in live-in domestic service for at least one year.

Though the Scheme was abandoned in the late 1960s, certain components resurfaced (with slight variation) in all subsequent immigration policies up to the present. First, women are confined to live-in domestic work for a specified length of time as a condition of their immigration status. The rationale was (and is) that there is no shortage of live-out domestic workers in Canada. Thus, an instrument of government policy is used to keep women in the form of domestic labour that renders them most vulnerable to the worst exploitation.

The requirement imposed under the Scheme that women be single and without dependants disclosed a resolute antipathy toward women migrants of colour who might someday attempt to settle in Canada, sponsor their families, and become permanent additions to Canadian society. The requirement that women have no family commitments also comports with the possessive nature of a master–servant relation. Rosanna Hertz (1986:162) notes that young immigrant women were popular among American employers in the early twentieth century because "they did not have local kinship ties of their own that could foster dual loyalties." Writing about contemporary practice in Colombia, where domestic workers often migrate from rural to urban areas, Bertha Quintero (Garcia Castro 1989:119) observes that, "[t]he attempt is made, although not always in a direct manner, to have the woman who works as a live-in domestic break all affective ties to her former life and become the property of her new family."

The advent of the Caribbean Domestic Scheme also marked the gradual transition from a predominantly white labour pool in domestic service to one in which the majority were women of colour. Though Canada did not have a specific legacy of Black enslavement or the "southern mammy" tradition, beliefs about the inferiority of non-whites took root and flourished here as they did in all Anglo-European colonial offspring. The degraded status of domestic work and of non-whites proved mutually reinforcing as women of colour became identified with the occupation. Agnes Calliste (1991:106) reports that while employers found Caribbean domestic workers "more educated, 'fond of children,' obliging and less demanding than other domestics," they also paid Caribbean workers up to $150 less per month than their white counterparts (1991:149). The notion that women of colour are at once uniquely well suited to domestic service yet (or perhaps *therefore*) worth less money than white women is a recurring paradox.

After a brief period of relatively open migration by domestic workers, in 1973, the Canadian government instituted a system of temporary work visas for domestic workers. The visas stipulated that the holder could remain in Canada only as long as she was employed as a domestic worker. The visas could be renewed annually but the domestic worker had no genuine prospect of converting her status from visitor to immigrant and ultimately to citizen.

The visa system effectively transformed domestic workers into a class of disposable migrant labourers, not unlike European "guest workers." (The institution of guest workers is relatively uncommon in Canada; the only other designated group are seasonal farm labourers.) This was a very economical and efficient system for Canada—the domestic worker's labour power was produced at the expense of the sending country and extracted in Canada in the form of childcare, housework, and cooking. If she lost her job she could be deported.[2] Domestic workers under the employment visa program were cheap, exploitable, and expendable.

And exploited they were—economically, physically, and sexually. The threat of dismissal and deportation, a spectre which employers and government officials capitalized upon at will, silenced these women, effaced their suffering, and gave employers what they wanted—a passive, cheap, compliant labour force. During this period, however, various Black, immigrant, and women's organizations began to agitate on behalf of domestic workers. Domestic workers themselves organized nationwide to protest their treatment by employers and government alike (Epstein 1983:228, 236). Horrific tales of abuse at the hands of employers (including government officials[3]) and immigration authorities garnered media attention, especially during the highly publicized case of the "seven Jamaican women." The case began in 1977 when immigration officials attempted to deport seven women admitted as immigrants several years earlier under the Caribbean Domestic Scheme. The women had failed to list their dependent children on their applications to immigrate (since that would have barred them from entry to Canada) and were discovered in 1976 when they attempted to sponsor their supposedly non-existent children.

The campaign to fight the deportation of the seven Jamaican women grew into a broader struggle to encompass domestic workers on temporary work visas. Under the rallying cry "good enough to work, good enough to stay," domestic workers voiced their demand for the same opportunity to immigrate extended to others whose labour was socially necessary and in high demand. The campaign culminated in changes to federal policy in late 1981 to permit foreign domestic workers to apply for landed-immigrant status from within Canada under a scheme entitled the Foreign Domestic Movement (FDM) Program.

Foreign Domestic Movement (FDM) Program: Relocating the Domestic Worker Inside the Law

The Program

Under the FDM Program, a foreign domestic worker who completed two years of live-in work in Canada could apply and be considered for landed-immigrant status from within Canada. There was no guarantee of acceptance, but the opportunity to apply was an improvement over the temporary visa system. Until such time as a foreign domestic worker did acquire landed-immigrant status however, she was still regarded as a temporary visitor on a work visa. (The practical difference between being a visitor and a landed immigrant is that visitors may only remain in Canada temporarily, whereas immigrants have a presumptive right to reside permanently in Canada and eventually acquire citizenship.)

The major qualification for admission under the FDM Program was ✓ that an applicant possess a minimum of one year's fulltime experience as a domestic worker or a certificate from a recognized school showing successful completion of a domestic worker training program. An example of the latter would be the National Nursery Examination Board (NNEB) course offered in Britain.

The FDM Program formally repudiated the absolute prohibition on applicants who were married and/or mothers, but maintained marital and family status as relevant factors in the selection process. The *Immigration Manual* instructed visa officers as follows:

> The fact that applicants may be married and/or have dependants should be considered in relation to their background and work history and the eventual self-sufficiency of the family unit; however, applications should not be refused only on the basis that the applicant has dependants. (*Immigration Manual*, IS 15.61)

The policy was ambiguous at best, and anecdotal evidence substantiated rumours of the routine rejection of applicants with spouses and/or children (Petrykanyn 1989:3). One woman recalls her initial rejection from the FDM Program by a visa officer: "She was telling me, 'Your job wouldn't be able to support your family.' I agreed with her but I had no intention of bringing my children at that time. I told her of my options, that maybe I could do better than domestic work in the future" (Flavelle 1990:

18

C6). On the advice of recruitment agencies, some applicants lied about being married or having children in order to secure acceptance into the FDM Program. As with the "seven Jamaican women" case, misrepresentation generated serious legal complications for those women who subsequently applied for landed-immigrant status.

Women accepted into the FDM Program and their future employers signed Employer-Employee Agreements furnished by Canada Employment and Immigration. The document set out wages, hours of work, duties, and days off. The agreement typically stipulated a forty- to fifty-hour work week at the minimum hourly wage prevailing in the employer's province of residence. Legislated employment standards fall within provincial jurisdiction and vary from one region to another. Some provinces exclude domestic workers entirely from minimum wage, maximum hours, and overtime protection. Others provide domestic workers with lesser protections than ordinary workers, such as a lower hourly wage or a weekly rather than hourly wage with no overtime pay. Only Ontario and Manitoba guarantee an hourly minimum wage and overtime pay.[4] The terms of the Employer-Employee Agreement drafted by the immigration department differed from one province to the next and occasionally exceeded the minimum employment standards applicable to domestic workers in that province.[5]

After completing two years of domestic work, a domestic worker on the FDM Program could apply for permission to immigrate. She would be assessed under a variety of criteria designed to determine whether she "has, or is reasonably likely to become successfully established and self-sufficient" in Canada ("Evaluation of Domestics for Landing in Canada," *Immigration Manual*, IE 9.16, Appendix C). Three factors were critical: first, successful employment history as a domestic worker; second, evidence of skills upgrading; third (and once again), the existence of dependent family members.

Proof of a successful employment record consisted of favourable reports from employers and long-term employment with one or two employers over the two year period. Skills upgrading usually involved taking evening courses to learn a trade other than domestic work. The upgrading requirement seemed anomalous to some, considering that employers expressed genuine consternation at the rate domestic workers exited the occupation at the first available opportunity. The explanation for the government's policy lay in its overriding concern that no future immigrant become a financial burden on the state. Since domestic labour was so cheap, the government feared that domestic workers would be unable to support themselves and/or any dependants they might eventually sponsor if they remained in the occupation. Of course, the irony is that domestic work paid so little in part because the FDM Program created a captive labour force who could not leave the occupation for a fixed period of time on pain of deportation. Workers in this situation were hardly in any position to bargain for better wages, especially when the government could manipulate the short-term supply of domestic workers to increase competition.

Thus, the government's own policy toward domestic workers facilitated their departure from the occupation by linking job retraining to acceptance as an immigrant. In a real sense, it was not "domestic workers" who were accepted as immigrants; rather, it was women who were domestic workers but were also on their way to becoming something else who were admitted into the Canadian community.

The third factor to be considered for landing, the existence of dependent family members, was canvassed earlier in the context of selection criteria. Here it re-emerged to catch women who might have misrepresented their marital or family status upon entry. It may also be understood as being premised on the same concern as the upgrading requirement, namely, future self-sufficiency. Upgrading proceeded from the recognition that domestic labour—the ultimate example of "women's work"—is too poorly paid to support a family. The dependent family members criteria generalized from "women's work" to women themselves, and presumed that women—whatever they do—cannot perform in the role of sole or primary head of a household. It also assumed that domestic workers, once admitted as immigrants, would immediately proceed to sponsor their dependants without regard to their ability to support them.

In sum, the basic contours of the FDM Program were as follows: First, overseas applicants had to have experience or academic training as a live-in domestic worker. Second, while in Canada, they were not protected by the same employment standards as other workers. Third, domestic workers faced deportation if they left the occupation (even to perform domestic work on a live-out basis) within two years. Fourth, their acceptance as a landed immigrant was conditioned by criteria intended to measure their ability to successfully establish in Canada. A good employment record was important. Having a spouse and/or dependants made one a less attractive candidate for admission to the program and ultimately immigration. Learning another skill during one's term was an advantage.

What Became of the Women

To understand how the FDM Program worked, and more particularly how it operated differently on women from different backgrounds, it is necessary to identify the demographic composition of the migrant women.

Since the inception of the FDM Program in 1982, the total number of women admitted as domestic workers increased from approximately thirty-five hundred in 1983 to almost eleven thousand in 1990 (Canada Employment and Immigration 1991). The surge in demand was attributable to the rise in dual–career families, a phenomenon which will be discussed in the next section. During this period, the actual numbers of British and European participants increased only slightly, while the numbers of Caribbean entrants declined somewhat. By 1990, British and European workers represented approximately 20 percent of the total number of new entrants, while the share of Caribbean women dropped from a peak of 20 percent in 1984 to 4.7 percent in 1991 (Canada Employment and Immigration 1992:2). A dramatic rise in Filipina entrants to the FDM Program accounted for the bulk of the increase. Today, the Philippines surpasses all other regions as the predominant country of origin for foreign domestic workers in Canada. In 1983, only 15 percent of entrants were Filipina; in 1991 they comprised 68 percent of program participants. Certain characteristics of migrant workers from Less Developed Countries (LDCs) (such as the Philippines) distinguish them from their Anglo-European counterparts. Most obvious among these is race: Virtually all Anglo-European domestic workers are white; Filipina domestic workers are not. If race is to have any explanatory force in this context however, it is only as a visual metonym for national origin and culture, which are variously deployed as indices of certain predispositions and propensities attributed to domestic workers of colour.

A particularly stark example of the encoding of hierarchy onto the domestic worker population is visible in the labelling process employed by recruitment agencies to classify domestic workers according to where they come from (DeVan 1989:87)[6]:

> I think if you were talking about a Filipino you would probably use the term domestic, and if you were talking about Australia, New Zealand it's nanny housekeeper, and if you were talking about a plain nanny it's someone who only does the work for the children. If it was me they [employers] were talking to they would definitely know the difference because if you hired somebody that's an NNEB [National Nursery Examination Board] from Britain and you ask her to do the housework she's not going to do it for you.

> ... when a family wants a very professional, trained nanny they will hire an English nanny, but they can't expect a lot of housekeeping. When they want somebody who will do light housekeeping, tidying, maybe preparing the evening meal, and

lots of childcare they'll hire a European. If they want somebody who can do all the housekeeping and maybe they have babies or small children they'll hire the Filipinos.

Consider the paradox: The more "professional" the domestic worker, the less labour she is expected to perform in addition to childcare. It cannot be that British women are incapacitated from housework on account of their training, nor is it obvious that Filipina domestic workers are so much more efficient and energetic that they can do the work of a nanny and all the housekeeping in a normal working day. Rather, it would appear that the further the domestic worker departs from the stereotypic image of Mary Poppins (linguisitically and physically), the more employers are encouraged to "compensate" for the apparent deficit by extracting additional labour from the worker.

Another critical move in legitimating the subordination of women of colour in domestic work is to attribute to them a "natural" affinity for domestic labour which women of the preferred race allegedly do not share. Consider the following depictions of Filipina domestic workers by recruitment agencies (DeVan 1989:88-89):

> They're . . . great with kids. They really like small children. They're very loving, they're very calm. A lot of families though with older children don't want Filipinos because Filipinos have a problem with discipline. They're too loving, they're not firm enough with the kids, but with young families they're great and so they have a big demand.

> Filipino people stay the longest. They don't go out at night, they're not as social. Young girls from Europe are lively. . . . It's a quieter living girl [sic] in your home, and not only that, they're better housekeepers and laundresses.

> Filipinos, you could eat off the floor, they're that clean. For some people that's a priority. Filipinos as a rule are very quiet people. They would not get overly friendly with and, um, get friends with the extended family members and all that.

> The Filipinos tend to be quite domesticated in their upbringing . . . it's their whole nature. They are a little more subservient, whether families want to treat them like that or not it's their whole nature—some families like that—they like to know that they are going to have someone who's going to be hard working.

Filipina women, then, are "naturally" domesticated, good with children, born housekeepers, and subservient. On this reasoning, employers do not exploit the Filipina domestic by extracting labour from them that they would not ask of (or get from) a British nanny; rather, employers merely ask her to do what comes "naturally" to Asian women.[7]

What external factors might explain why Filipina domestic workers are described as uniquely diligent and compliant? First, as Lycklama (1989) indicates, women from LDCs often migrate in order to earn money they can remit to dependants in the home country. This would not be the usual pattern for foreign domestic workers from Developed Countries (DCs). The Filipina worker will thus be conscious that others rely on her wages for support, whereas the British worker has only herself to worry about.

Yet another difference between the two groups relates to the means of acquiring qualifications for domestic work. Filipina domestic workers most frequently qualify on the basis of experience rather than formal training in domestic work. A typical route of entry would involve a period of work in either Singapore, Hong Kong or, less commonly, the Middle East, prior to applying to Canada. Domestic workers in these countries are often expected to do everything and anything the employers demand; working conditions for domestic workers in these countries are reputedly abysmal.[8]

In contrast to this dismal experience, British women applying to the FDM Program frequently qualified on the basis of a certificate from the NNEB, which promotes respect for childcare as a skilled occupation and encourages students to resist attempts by employers to add housekeeping tasks to their childcare duties.

Perhaps *the* critical distinguishing feature between women from LDCs and Anglo-European women is that the former frequently have a greater interest in immigrating to Canada. According to one recruitment agency representative,

> The majority of girls out of Europe come here for a year and they're out. [They] go back to university and get on with their lives. But the girls from third world countries, like the Philippines, are here hoping to have the opportunity to become Canadian. [Filipinas] . . . feel that they are upgrading their life style and they can send money home. It is with the goal of coming to Canada and becoming a landed immigrant and being able to sponsor their family. (DeVan 1989:83-84)

To illustrate the impact of this immigration factor, consider a scenario where the employer is not paying the domestic worker overtime wages. Studies suggest that domestic workers usually work ten to eleven hours daily, and sometimes longer. Surveys conducted in British Columbia (West Coast DWA 1990:4) and Ontario (INTERCEDE 1990:6) indicate that employers paid no wages whatsoever for overtime work (much less time-and-a-half) in 63 percent and 44 percent of cases respectively. Recalling that "domestics" are expected to work harder (and presumably longer) than "nannies," the failure to pay overtime effectively depresses the hourly wage of Filipina women relative to their white counterparts.

In Ontario, provincial law entitles domestic workers to overtime pay after forty-four hours. In theory, a domestic worker could complain to the local employment standards branch that the employer was not paying overtime as required by law. In reality however, workers rarely lodge complaints regarding on-going employment situations. The prospects are even dimmer where the employee is new to the country, fearful of government officials, and lives in the home of her employer. Her employers are Canadian, she is not. They are wealthy, she is not. They are native English or French speakers, she is not. She is dependent on them not only for a job, but also for room, board, and her presence in Canada. As one government official concedes:

> How can you go on working? How can you go on living side-by-side with somebody when you've suddenly appeared on opposite sides of a referee . . . . [V]ery few of us live and work in the same place and far fewer of us work in the employer's house. They can't get away from each other. It's a very difficult relationship. (Klein 1990)

In most other provinces, the domestic worker could not seek protection under provincial employment standards legislation because she could be excluded from the relevant overtime provision. Alternatively, she could try to fall back on her Employer-Employee Agreement if it contained an overtime provision. Once more, the likelihood of a domestic worker attempting to enforce her contract in court was virtually nil. Canada Employment and Immigration, which supplied the contract in the first place, always took the inexplicable and probably indefensible view that the contract was not legally enforceable. In the result, she could expect no help from immigration officials in persuading a recalcitrant employer to pay her overtime. The Employer-Employee Agreement was effectively meaningless except as an exhortation to employers not to exploit their domestic workers.

As a last resort, a domestic worker under the FDM Program also had the option of changing employers, but the mobility of domestic workers was regulated and constrained by the terms of the program. Unlike ordinary workers, foreign domestic workers had to obtain permission from an immigration officer before switching employers. The *Immigration Manual* stated that a domestic worker could change employers for various reasons, such as economic improvement, personality clash with the employer, or the failure of either party to "live up to the other's expectations" (Canada Employment and Immigration *Immigration Manual* IE-9, 9.16(7)). A domestic worker wishing to change employers was asked to produce a "release letter" from her current employer commenting on "the quality of the domestic's work and the reason for leaving her employment" (*Immigration Manual* IE 9.16(7)(b)). Some employers resented the domestic worker's decision to leave and simply refuse to supply the letter, and one domestic worker recalled being threatened with deportation when she requested one from her employers (Stainsby 1989). In the absence of a release letter, immigration officials contacted employers directly to investigate the domestic worker's competence, conduct, and reasons for leaving. In cases of conflict, domestic workers suspected that immigration officials consistently took the employers' word over theirs. In one case where the domestic worker and the employers gave discrepant versions of their relationship, the immigration officer allegedly asked the domestic worker, "Why should I believe a foreigner over two Canadian citizens?" (West Coast DWA 1990b:16).

Though domestic workers were rarely denied permission to change employers, they were tacitly discouraged from doing so. As noted earlier, an important factor in a domestic worker's assessment for landed-immigrant status was a satisfactory employment record over the two years. More than three employers in two years could jeopardize a woman's chances of success. This was the perception of domestic workers and of organizations representing their interests. A woman who planned to go back to England in a year or two might not care what effect challenging her employer's authority or even switching employers might have on her ability to immigrate; a woman who desperately needed the job to support her family in the Philippines and who hoped to settle in Canada permanently might assess the stakes differently, and behave accordingly.

At some level, employers knew this, and so did the employment agencies:

> The chances of having them fill their contractual obligations are much better, uh, the Filipino and Jamaican women, because most of them, 99.99 percent of them are working towards a future in Canada. They will be more loyal and more conscientious. (DeVan 1989:89)

. . . And more compliant, and less likely to complain. And more vulnerable to abuse. What looks like "natural" subservience or an unbounded penchant for housework may reflect nothing more than capitulation to short-term abuse in exchange for a shot at the prize of long-term membership:

> Right now I get $710 a month, which is what I am suppose to get as Manpower say. But when I took the job, I wasn't told that I was suppose to clean and wash clothes too for that money. I am afraid to go and complain to Manpower, because this is my third job, and they watch this sort of thing, so maybe if I go and complain they might tell me to go home. They might think I am a troublemaker. (Silvera 1990:59)[9]

In summary, the construction of the foreign domestic worker under the FDM Program as a passive, exploitable entity was facilitated by the state in key respects. First, the live-in requirement imposed by the scheme potentiated exploitation; second, domestic workers' exclusion from, or inferior status within employment standards legislation reinforced the notion that domestic work is not "real" work and, by extension, the people who do it deserve less respect and protection than "real" employees. The refusal by immigration officials to treat the Employer-Employee Agreement as an enforceable contract further trivialized the domestic worker's status as employee, insulated the profound inequality of power between domestic worker and employer from state intervention, and left the domestic worker's welfare wholly at the disposition of the employer. Finally, the constant fear of deportation rendered women from Less Developed Countries particularly susceptible to exploitation. In effect, the FDM Program did less to mitigate the vulnerability of domestic workers than to relocate it within the boundaries of law.

Live-in Caregiver Program (LCP): Creating More Zoë Bairds?
On January 30, 1992, Bernard Valcourt, then Minister of Employment and Immigration, imposed a moratorium on the processing of foreign domestic workers who had not yet been approved for entry into Canada. On April 27, 1992, Valcourt introduced several changes to the scheme, including a new name: the Live-in Caregiver Program (LCP).

Under the initial terms of the LCP, applicants from abroad had to demonstrate completion of "a course of study that is the equivalent of Canadian grade twelve" and "six months of full-time formal training in a field or occupation" related to the specific type of caregiving position sought. The first stipulation responded to the concern that live-in domestic workers often leave the occupation after obtaining permanent resident status, and labour force projections for Canada indicate that 65 percent of new jobs in Canada in the next ten years will require at least a twelfth grade education (Canada Employment and Immigration 1993). The six month training requirement represented yet another attempt to "professionalize" the occupation of live-in domestic work without furnishing any financial or other incentives to actually transform it into a higher-status occupation that is attractive to workers over the long term.

The LCP appears more flexible than its predecessor with respect to the type of formal training that may qualify as related to a caregiving occupation (that is, childcare, senior home support care, or care of the disabled). These requirements have been enacted in the form of amendments to the *Immigration Regulations*.[10]

The requirement that domestic workers obtain "release letters" from their employer prior to switching employers has been abolished, though employers will be obligated to provide a departing employee with a Record of Employment (ROE) showing how many weeks the domestic worker was employed and a statement of her earnings. The domestic worker may lodge a complaint with the Canada Employment Centre if the employer refuses to issue an ROE.

With respect to the criteria for landing, the domestic worker must only demonstrate a minimum of two years employment as a fulltime live-in domestic worker. There is no longer any requirement to show skills upgrading.

Finally, the government has undertaken to provide domestic workers with "counselling information outlining terms and conditions of employment and their rights under Canadian laws" and has pledged that the "counselling role of domestic workers' advocacy groups will be supported and encouraged"(Canada Employment and Immigration 1992:1-2). Canada Employment and Immigration has also published a new guide entitled, "The Live-in Caregiver Program: Information for Employers and Live-in Caregivers from Abroad" (Canada, Ministry of Supply and Services 1992) which sets out the terms of the LCP with respect to selection abroad, general rights and responsibilities with respect to the workplace, and the requirements for landing.

Because the LCP is new, data about its effect on the number, composition, and treatment of domestic workers are largely anecdotal. To the extent that the LCP retains the mandatory "live-in" component, the essential nature of the occupation is unlikely to change dramatically, though the government's commitment to furnishing domestic workers with counselling and information may, if undertaken diligently, reduce the incidence of abuse and exploitation.

Taken in isolation, the relaxing of criteria for landing seems highly commendable. The overall effect of the new scheme, however, has been to raise the standards for initial entry to "compensate" for this slackening of the landing criteria. This shift in emphasis appears to be having a disproportionately negative impact on women applying from Less Developed Countries (LDCs), such as the Philippines and the Caribbean nations.

The original terms of the LCP required that applicants have at least six months of formal training in a caregiving occupation. Under the FDM Program, applicants could qualify on the basis of formal training or practical experience. As noted earlier, British domestic workers frequently came equipped with certification from the National Nursery Examination Board, whereas the vast majority of women from LDCs entered on the basis of their experience. Under the original terms of the LCP, this would no longer be possible: The guidelines for the implementation of the LCP unequivocally declare that "[t]raining does not mean experience. Therefore, practical experience, in whole or in part, which is not part of a formal training program or course, does not qualify as a substitute for training."[11] Though the LCP guidelines suggest a flexible approach to determining whether a training program or course is related to caregiving, they are unlikely to loosen the constrictive impact of the training requirement to any meaningful degree.

Consider also the requirement that applicants possess the equivalent of a Canadian grade twelve education. Statistics produced by Employment and Immigration indicate that 44 percent of Filipina domestic workers and 49 percent of Caribbean domestic workers approved for permanent residence in 1989 did not have twelve years of schooling, compared to 22 percent of British women (Canada Employment and Immigration 1991). Thus, the new educational requirements would have effectively excluded almost one third of the current pool of foreign domestic workers. Moreover, the requirement of grade twelve seems unrelated to the question of whether applicants possess the skills necessary to perform domestic work. It is even questionable whether it is relevant to the future economic performance of the women who leave domestic work after landing, since the educational attainments of women educated abroad are frequently discounted in the Canadian job market anyway (Ng 1987:30-31). It is worth noting in this context that fully 37 percent of Filipina domestic workers had some post secondary education, ranging from the undergraduate to the doctoral level (Canada Employment and Immigration 1991).

To the extent that the new LCP would eliminate significant numbers of women from the pool of eligible applicants, it raised the question of whether the stricter criteria would permit the entry of enough domestic workers to satisfy employer demands. The number of women admitted to Canada in 1992 as part of the FDM Program backlog or under the new LCP totalled only 3,878, or half of the 7,835 admitted under the FDM Program in 1991 (Canada Employment and Immigration 1993). Preliminary and anecdotal evidence (Mitchell 1993:A5; McLeans 1993, 40) suggested that the LCP was not bringing in enough workers to meet demand[12], with the result that a parallel shadow market comprised of illegal domestic workers is emerging. While the domestic workers admitted under the LCP will enjoy greater protection than their FDM predecessors, another new "underclass" of illegal domestic workers may find themselves in as precarious a position as their American counterparts.

On June 9, 1993, the Minister of State for Employment and Immigration tabled a recommendation that the regulation setting out the terms of the LCP be amended to restore the one year's experience in caregiving as an alternative to the six month's formal training criterion. In other words, it would appear that the LCP criteria were indeed too stringent to meet employer demand; restoring the one year experience alternative will remove one of the main obstacles to admission, though the grade twelve equivalency remains in place. Almost a year later, the new Liberal government adopted the recommendation and amended the *Immigration Regulations* to make one year's experience an acceptable alternative to six-months training.[13]

The United States, unlike Canada, does not have a formal program for importing domestic workers. As Romero indicates in chapter two, the availability of American workers to perform live-in domestic labour has been in steady decline for several years. Martha Giminez (1990:41-42) posits a linkage between this phenomenon and current lobbying for live-out childcare in the United States: "The demand for childcare itself reflects the options open to a society in which an ideological commitment to political equality makes the call for more and affordable servants a political impossibility." If the Zoë Baird episode has revealed anything, it is that the call for more and affordable servants in the United States is less impossible than merely *unnecessary*. The United States borders are sufficiently porous to permit employers to find numerous undocumented Latina, Caribbean, and other migrant women willing to do live-in work.[14]

The presence of these women is illegal. They can be deported any time. In theory, it is also illegal for employers to hire undocumented aliens and such employers are subject to fines and penalties. That is, it was illegal for Zoë Baird and her spouse to employ Lillian Cordero and her spouse because the couple were so-called undocumented aliens. In reality however, the Immigration and Naturalization Service (INS) refrains from investigating employers of domestic workers. Employers who behave in exactly the same manner as did Zoë Baird, with the tacit complicity of the INS, probably number in the tens (if not hundreds) of thousands. The fact that the INS will not enforce the employer sanction against employers of live-in domestic workers makes the occupation more attractive to un-documented workers since it reduces the likelihood of detection. The corollary is that live-in domestic workers become even more vulnerable to exploitation by employers, who can implicitly, explicitly, or even unwittingly use the threat of deportation to intimidate, exploit, and abuse them. After all, the employer of an undocumented domestic worker need not fear penalties for hiring her, but the worker herself still faces the very real likelihood of deportation if she is reported to the INS.

Despite their illegal status in the United States, undocumented domestic workers are nevertheless included under federal employment standards laws, including minimum wage, overtime, and maximum hours. Employers are required to remit Social Security taxes, unemploy-ment insurance premiums, and related payments to the government in respect of employees, even if they are breaking the law by employing them in the first place. Not surprisingly, many employers flout the employment laws relating to domestic workers. Fear of deportation inhibits domestic workers from complaining;[15] economic desperation precludes them from leaving the job or the country voluntarily. When Zoë Baird and her spouse hired the Corderos, they were tapping into a community of labourers they could count on to "work hard and work scared."

Feminist Implications

The demand for live-in workers has escalated dramatically over the last twenty years. The trend is directly attributable to the rise in North American women's participation in the workforce, particularly in the professions. Zoë Baird epitomizes this phenomenon, though it would be fair to say that scant numbers of women (or men for that matter) earn the half a million dollar salary that she did.

Women's entry into the higher paying occupations has not materially altered other aspects of their lives, however. First, many women still want to have children. Second, whether they parent alone or with another, women still bear primary responsibility for child rearing and domestic labour (Hochschild 1989). Third, the professional workplace is still organized around a male breadwinner/female housewife model that demands long hours at the office and a commitment to work that presumes someone else is taking care of the kids and the home. Given these conditions, working parents face an intractable dilemma, namely, how to meet the demands of career and nuclear family without sacrificing either. Enter the live-in domestic worker:

> . . . both husband and wife are out there supporting the mortgage and . . . have babies as well. They all have to have a nanny or otherwise they can't work. Either it's live-in or it's live-out or it's daycare . . . live-out costs more. The difference with daycare is that nobody does your housework. You have to drop the kids off, and you can't be late coming home from the office or go and meet your husband for dinner. You can phone your nanny and say we're going to be an hour or two late and would you please take care of the kiddies. (Employment Agency Representative, quoted in DeVan 1989:72)

One accountant states her position succinctly, "Almost all of my friends have nannies. In my profession, it's very difficult to use daycare. . . . I need the flexibility (Flavelle 1990:C5). Of course, one woman's flexibility can be another woman's straitjacket:

> I'd say my day started at about 7:30 in the morning when the kids got up and I would work until about 6:00 p.m. when my employers came home from work, but that depended from day to day, because sometimes they came home later. They just took it for granted that I didn't have anyplace to go, even though they never asked me if I had anywhere to go. (Silvera 1990:26)

There is a certain temptation, especially for a feminist, to label the domestic worker a "surrogate housewife." After all, domestic workers are hired to perform the tasks assigned to the modern housewife. The social and physical isolation, the invisibility of the work, the physical labour, and the interminable nature of the tasks go with the job, no matter who performs it. From a stark economic perspective, the domestic worker is a surrogate housewife who is nominally better off because she is paid for her labour. Equating the domestic worker to a housewife permits one to subsume the oppression of the domestic worker into an analysis of women's oppression *qua* wife and mother. The label is convenient because of its contemporary referent, but the analogy is wrong. The persona of a domestic worker, even in her "mothering" capacity, owes little to the role of middle-class, twentieth-century housewife. She is neither a substitute mother nor a substitute wife. She is the modern incarnation of the pre-industrial servant.

When employers insist that a domestic worker is "like one of the family," they unwittingly affirm the feudal quality of the relation. At no time was the domestic worker more like "one of the family" than when her status was formally acknowledged to be that of a servant: Prior to the Industrial Revolution, household and family were synonymous and coextensive (Rollins 1985:26-7) and functioned as an integrated economic unit of production (Nicholson 1984:82). Servants living under the master's roof were considered full members in the patriarchal household (Coser 1973:31). The world inhabited by the servant did not treat the family and the market as mutually exclusive categories. It is the historical roots of live-in servitude that accounts for the difficulty of mapping the reality of domestic workers' experience onto contemporary public/ private discourse. Privileging a definition of the household as private, and thus immune from both market behaviour and state intervention, effectively effaces the domestic worker's identity as an employee in a workplace.

The role of the foreign domestic worker is not merely anomalous; it is anachronistic. In a sense, the contradictions inhere in the very label "foreign/domestic/worker": though she is technically foreign, she is also enmeshed in the domestic, economic and legal machinery of Canada far more deeply than a mere visitor. She is a worker, yet her work (and her person) remain invisible as long as they are confined to the "domestic" realm. She receives neither the full legal protection accorded employees, nor the emotional and affective benefits of family membership. As Sedef Arat-Koç (1989:39) declares, "Squeezed between the private and public spheres, she belongs to neither one, and probably combines the worst aspects of both."

Rather than define the domestic worker by analogy to a housewife, it might be more accurate to depict the middle-class housewife as the conflation of "two roles, the role of servant (primarily engaged in tasks of physical reproduction) and the role of 'lady of the house' (primarily engaged in management and tasks of social reproduction)" (Giminez 1990:40-1). The re-emergence of the domestic worker thus signifies the disentangling of those two roles and a resumption of the pre-Industrial bifurcation of mistress and servant among the middle and upper classes.

Even today, women who do not work outside the home are still able to derive status from their husbands. Conversely, the low status of the contemporary domestic worker appears impervious to the social position of her employers and is, in any case, lower than a housewife of any class (Bose 1980:76). After all, the oft invoked refrain that wives are glorified servants[16] derives its rhetorical force by appealing to a shared perception of the natural inferiority of servants.[17] Inverting the trope can only make the domestic worker's lot appear rosier than it really is.

Furthermore, many foreign domestic workers *are* wives and mothers whose own families have been dismembered by the exigencies of third world poverty and restrictive immigration laws. Assimilating the terms "wife" and "servant" elides this aspect of domestic worker's identity in much the same way as comparing the situation of women and Blacks obscures the existence of Black women (Spelman 1988:114-5). It also privileges the identification of the family as the primary site of all women's oppression by conflating the experience of oppression within *one's own* family with oppression by *someone else's* family. As Daiva Stasiulis (1987:5-6) remarks, many migrant women of colour experience this separation from their family as a greater source of suffering than the sex oppression occurring within a family unit:

> The central focus on the family as a site for women's oppression is regarded as highly problematic for black feminists. They argue that in racist societies, the family has provided opportunities for egalitarian relations among women and men, and has functioned as a site for shelter and resistance. Black feminists also decry the focus of feminist theory on the centrality of the family in enforcing women's oppression, when racially restrictive immigration laws have served to destroy black families by separating husbands from wives, wives from husbands, and parents from children. . . . The distinct relationship of non-white, non-European women to the state has been encoded in a patchwork of racist immigration policies which actively restricted the entry into Canada of dependants of male or female non-white migrant workers.

From a feminist perspective, the most glaring and problematic reason for resisting the fusion of wife and servant is that it is most frequently the woman of the household who directly supervises the domestic worker. Adopting an analytical approach that asks a domestic worker to identify her oppression with that of her employer insults her lived experience.[18] It also ignores the way domestic service functions to reinforce social hierarchy along other dimensions of inequality:

> The presence of the "inferior" domestic, an inferiority evidenced by the performance she is encouraged to execute and her acceptance of demeaning treatment, offers the employer justification for materially exploiting the domestic, ego enhancement as an individual, and a strengthening of the employer's class and racial

identities. Even more important, such a presence supports the ideal of unequal human worth: it suggests that there might be categories of people (the lower classes, people of color) who are inherently inferior to others (middle and upper classes, whites). And this idea provides ideological justification for a social system that institutionalizes inequality. (Rollins 1985:203)

The grim truth is that some women's access to the high-paying, high-status professions is being facilitated through the revival of semi-indentured servitude. Put another way, one woman is exercising class and citizenship privilege to buy her way out of sex oppression. It is a measure of the personal success of some women that they are able to "make it" in a man's world on male terms. It is a measure of their failure on these same male terms that they will be blamed for the exploitation of domestic workers, for it signifies a tacit affirmation of the sexual division of labour: domestic workers do the "woman's work."

A Brazilian lawyer describes her own ambivalence about participating in the subordination of her family's domestic worker:

> [T]he domestic worker is a double, the other self one leaves at home doing those things that traditionally you, as a woman, should be doing . . . I felt it in my own flesh, this other self who freed me so that I could perform my other roles. At the beginning, I felt very guilty: guilt for having a domestic worker, guilt for exploiting another woman's work. But suddenly I began to question why I alone should be feeling guilty, as she is not working just for me, but for everybody in my house. This type of guilt is felt by most feminist women who have domestic workers because it seems a contradiction to be a feminist and to employ a domestic worker. But if there is guilt, it should be shared by the entire family—husband, wife and children—who are actually benefiting from somebody else's poorly paid work. (Pereira de Melo 1989:260-61)

As this passage suggests, the assertion of power by a female employer over another woman is constituted by and through the disempowerment she experiences in her external relations with a patriarchal world, specifically the sexual division of labour in the home and the male-centred workplace. On the one hand, patriarchy illicitly transforms the individual woman into the proxy for the nuclear family and assigns blame to her for domestic workers' exploitation. On the other hand, acknowledging this fact hardly absolves a woman of her share of responsibility and, more to the point, is cold comfort to the domestic worker herself.

A female employer's power and her (ab)use of it is problematic from a feminist perspective. Her various privileges cannot be rationalized as being entirely parasitic on a man's. She cannot be dismissed from a feminist analysis as "exceptional" in her power without eliminating the domestic worker as exceptional in her disempowerment. They are as interdependent in theory as they are in life.

That domestic workers in Canada are poor, disenfranchised, foreign women of colour is not a prerequisite to exploitation, but it can facilitate it. Though female employer and domestic worker share gender as a common attribute, they are separated by race, class, and citizenship. Each of these vectors exert their own force on the nature, trajectory, and distribution of power in society. They also permit one woman to objectify another in various ways that are influenced, but not precluded, by gender. For example, a female employer can hardly claim that her domestic worker is ideally suited to domestic work because she is a woman without impugning her own status, but she can fall back on *Filipina* women being "naturally" hard working, subservient, loyal, tidy housekeepers, and good with children. In this context, race, ethnicity and culture conjoin with sex to create a sub-category of women whose subordination other women can rationalize by projecting onto them the stereotypical "feminine" qualities that patriarchy has used against women generally. As bell hooks trenchantly observes, women can use their various privileges to distance themselves from the women they deliberately or unwittingly oppress while aligning themselves with the men whose power they seek. Speaking of race relations in the United States, she writes that,

> . . . white men have supported changes in the white woman's social standing only if there exists another female group to assume that role. Consequently, the white patriarch undergoes no radical change in his sexist assumption that woman is inherently inferor. He neither relinquishes his dominant position nor alters the patriarchal structure of society. He is however, able to convince many white women that fundamental changes in "woman's status" have occurred because he has successfully socialized her, via racism, to assume that no connection exists between her and black women. (hooks 1981:155)

In other words, employing a domestic worker does nothing to challenge the patriarchal organization of the home or the workplace. It simply changes the identity of the woman doing the "woman's work." From a feminist perspective, this solution has little to commend it. Having said that, it is worth pausing to speculate on what would happen if the government prohibited the importation of foreign domestic workers tomorrow. Various possibilities spring to mind: Perhaps employers would reconsider the legitimacy of the demands placed upon working women and restructure the workplace to accomodate the parenting responsibilities borne disproportionately by women. Perhaps men would begin to assume an equal responsibility for child rearing and housework so that these duties would no longer be borne disproportionately by women, and the workplace would reconfigure itself completely. Or consider this: neither of the above scenarios materialize and one parent (guess who?) has to return to the home, work part-time, or face being demoted, penalized, or otherwise marginalized for failing to live up to the demands of the job.

Assessing the likelihood of each of these scenarios provides a rough measure of the security women (even as professionals) actually enjoy in the workplace. A just solution to the dilemma of career and family would involve, at a minimum, equally distributing responsibility for child rearing across the sexes, whether within the nuclear family or through some other arrangement. It would also mean transfiguring the workplace and its priorities away from its anachronistic model of the male breadwinner with the stay-at-home housewife. Finally, it would require the state to assume a greater responsibility in making childcare available and affordable to all women and in paying those who do it a decent wage.

To resist the *status quo* governing home and workplace is to embark on a struggle that is daunting indeed. The odds of survival, much less victory, are slim. It is hardly surprising then that many women choose a path of lesser resistance: It will always be easier for Canadian women to foist the housework on a domestic worker than it will be to persuade men to do their share.[19] It will always be safer to take advantage of a domestic worker's "flexibility" than to antagonize bosses and senior colleagues by refusing to work late, or insisting that on-site daycare be a priority, or advocating that the firm's work ethic adapt to the presence of women who do not have "wives" at home.

As long as parents insist on having private, individualized childcare, employers of live-in domestic workers will have an incentive to keep domestic work as cheap (and socially devalued) as possible. Governments will not heed shopowners' complaints that paying clerks minimum wage and overtime will put them out of business, but they will listen to parents who say they cannot sustain their middle-class professional families unless they can overwork and underpay their domestic workers. The imperative of maintaining the family as a viable social, economic, and reproductive unit means that the dual—career nuclear family will continue to depend for its survival on the foreign domestic worker even as it, by definition, excludes her.

Finally, as long as the government can placate middle-class families by furnishing them with cheap foreign labour, immigration will be used to deflect and fragment the demand for affordable, accessible daycare. Couples who can afford the private solution will take it, leaving single, working-class, and poor mothers to cope with the government's broken promise to institute a universal daycare program.

Women like Zoë Baird who employ live-in domestic workers make constrained choices. They are caught between being subordinated as women and participating in the domination of other women. I do not purport to have the solution to this conflict. What I will say is that being a "good employer" does not vitiate one in maintaining the hierarchy of race, gender, and class relations that manifests globally between rich and poor countries, nationally in immigration laws, and domestically in households. Conscientious efforts to not capitalize on the exploitive potential of the domestic worker–employer relationship is a point of departure; it is not a destination.

Acknowledgement

Much of chapter one condenses material published earlier by the author in "Foreign Domestic Worker: Surrogate Housewife or Mail Order Servant?" (1992) 37 *McGill Law Journal* 681-760. The author wishes to thank Pearl Eliadis for sharing her insights and providing constructive criticism.

Notes

1. Zoë Baird was President Clinton's first nominee for Attorney General. She withdrew her candidacy when public furore erupted following her admission that she and her spouse had employed Lillian Cordero and her spouse, both undocumented aliens, as a live-in domestic worker and chauffeur respectively, contrary to an American law sanctioning employers who employ undocumented aliens. Ms. Baird and her spouse had also failed to pay Social Security and other related taxes in respect of the Corderos.

2. Estimates of the number of women who entered Canada on the Temporary Employment Authorization Program between 1973 and 1981 range from 27,000 to over 60,000. See Canada Employment and Immigration (Policy Branch) 1990; Estable (1986:30).

3. See Martin and Segrave (1985:123) for a 1979 incident involving Larry Grossman, then a Progressive Conservative cabinet minister in the Ontario government. He and his wife employed a domestic worker at less than the minimum wage. She allegedly worked fourteen to fifteen hours a day, and when she disclosed to them her illegal status, her work week was extended

from five and a half to seven days and her duties expanded to include laundering and house cleaning.

4. The right to overtime is qualified in both instances, however. In Ontario, employers of domestic workers may give time off in lieu of paying overtime; in Manitoba, a domestic worker is deemed to work no more than twelve hours daily.

5. For example, regulations passed pursuant to the British Columbia *Employment Standards Act* entitled domestic workers to a minimum of $40 per day in British Columbia, regardless of hours worked. The Employer-Employee Agreement furnished by Immigration Authorities in B.C. required employers to pay a minimum of $5/hour plus overtime pay after forty hours. On the other hand, the Nova Scotia *Labour Standards Code* excludes domestic workers entirely from any protection. The Employer-Employee Agreement used in Nova Scotia requires employers to pay the hourly minimum wage, but no mention is made of overtime.

6. The author acknowledges with gratitude the excellent primary research of Mary DeVan, whose M.A. thesis was of great assistance.

7. Worth noting in passing is Judith Rollins' (1989:180) observation that employers tacitly desire and expect subservience from domestic workers, and domestic workers supply it as deliberately and self-consciously as they do other services.

8. Recent accounts of mistreatment of foreign domestic workers in Kuwait exploded in the Western press following the American invasion of Iraq.

9. One story reported in the press concerned a woman who had changed employers three times and who was warned by an immigration officer that she would have to leave the country if she switched employers again. On the first day with her fourth employer, she was raped. She endured continued abuse for four months for fear of being deported if she tried to switch employers again (Imm Rev Worries DWs).

10. The regulations read as follows:

2(1) "Live-in caregiver" means a person who provides, without supervision, in a private household in Canada in which the person resides, child care, senior home support care or care of the disabled.

20(1.1) An immigration officer shall not issue an employment authorization to a person who seeks admission as a live-in caregiver unless the person:

    a.   has successfully completed a course of study that is the equivalent of Canadian grade twelve;

    b.   has successfully completed six months of full-time formal training in a field or occupation related to the employment for which the employment authorization is sought;

       i.   in a classroom setting, as part of the course of study referred to in paragraph (a) or otherwise, or;

      ii.   in a non-classroom setting where the training is part of a course of instruction given under the direction of a qualified educator or trainer who provides a rated assessment thereof; and;

    c.   has the ability to speak, read and understand English or French language at a level sufficient to communicate effectively in an unsupervised setting.

Immigration Regulations, 1978 as amended by SOR/92-214, P.C. 1992-685 (9 April 1992).

11. "Operations Memorandum," 4.41, 92-08, April 24, 1992, p. 5.

12. According to a newspaper source, only 779 Filipinas entered via the LCP in 1992. Another 126 came from Britain, and 22 from Jamaica. (Vivian Smith "Rules Yield to Need for Nannies" Globe and Mail, March 4, 1994: A1, A5).

13. See *Immigration Regulations, 1978* as amended by SOR/94-242, s.5. The "Regulatory Impact Analysis Statement" accompanying the amendment concedes that the original LCP criteria were too stringent. Only a thousand applicants qualified under the LCP in almost two years, or one-tenth the number accepted in the last full year of the FDM program (1991).

14. It is not clear what proportion of live-in domestic workers are illegal, since statistics about illegal workers are difficult to obtain for obvious reasons; informal estimates suggest, however, that the majority of live-in domestic workers in the United States are illegal.

15. Given how low wages are however, the failure of employers to deduct and remit Social Security taxes is often the least of domestic workers' concerns. It is ironic that this breach became the focus of so much attention in Zoë Baird's case.

16. As in Lady Chudleigh's 1703 quip: "Wife and servant are the same/but only differ in the name."

17. bell hooks makes a similar point with respect to white feminists comparing the lot of women to that of slaves and people of colour:

> Just as 19th century white woman's rights advocates attempt to make synonymous their lot with that of the black slave was aimed at drawing attention away from the slave toward themselves, contemporary white feminsts have used the same metaphor to attract attention to their concerns. . . . When white women talked about "Women as Niggers," "the Third World of Women," "Woman as Slave," they evoked the sufferings and oppressions of non-white people to say "look at how bad our lot as white women is, why we are like niggers, like the Third World." . . . [I]f they had been poor and oppressed, or women concerned about the lot of oppressed women, they would not have been compelled to appropriate the black experience. It would have been sufficient to describe the oppression of woman's experience. A white woman who has suffered physical abuse and assault from a husband or lover, who also suffers poverty, need not compare her lot to that of a suffering black person to emphasize that she is in pain (bell hooks 1991:142).

18. Writing about the American experience, bell hooks notes that "In the white community, employing domestic help was a sign of material privilege and the person who directly benefitted from a servant's work was the white woman, since without the servant she would have performed domestic chores. Not surprisingly, the black female domestic tended to see the white female as her 'boss', her oppressor, not the white male whose earnings usually paid her wage" (bell hooks 1981:155).

19. Many women report that they use domestic workers to avoid confrontations with their uncooperative partners (Arat-Koç 1989:43).

CHAPTER TWO

CHICANAS AND THE CHANGING WORK EXPERIENCE IN DOMESTIC SERVICE

Mary Romero

S ociologists, anthropologists, and historians define domestic service as a "peculiar occupation." Not only has the occupation continued for centuries, it appears to have survived the transformations of various economic systems—slavery, feudalism, and capitalism. To account for its persistence some researchers perceive domestic service as a remnant of premodern or preindustrial social formations. They treat the occupation's peculiarities as simply the vestigial remains of slavery and feudalism. While some researchers view domestic service as a vanishing occupation, others have suggested new trends that may transform paid housework.

Julie Matthaei (1982:282) argues that domestic service is a "vestige of the family economy within capitalism," and claims that working mothers no longer need private household workers. In part, her argument is based on the claim that commodities, labour-saving devices, and the reallocation of household tasks to family members eliminates the need for household workers. Lewis Coser (1974) made a similar argument on the basis that the occupation was becoming extinct because household labour has changed and the work is no longer useful in an industrialized and developed economy. Furthermore, he viewed modern employers as having different needs from their predecessors, needs that can be fulfilled without the personal service provided by private household workers. Lewis Coser, David Chaplin (1978), and others maintained that neither the Victorian aristocratic servant role nor the mistress and maid hierarchical relationship was consistent with our democratic society. Numerous researchers have suggested that the decline in household help reflected workers' refusal to engage in servitude and "is evidence of a change in the American character" (Levenstein 1962:38).

However, research on the experiences of women of colour working for white women in domestic service shows strong evidence that the personal service and deferential behavior, characteristic of the occupation in yesteryear, is still common. Furthermore, the statistics do not necessarily support the vanishing occupation thesis, but instead reflect the occupation's adaptation to America's late twentieth-century family structure. The shift to day work made it possible for domestics to work for more than one employer. Today, most private household workers are employed in a different home every day of the week. Since most of the wages are unreported to the U.S. Internal Revenue Service (IRS), firm statistics are not available. However, a recent estimate indicated that 43 percent of employed women hired household workers (Kleinman 1986).

Inquiries about the changing structure of domestic service become more important in understanding contemporary working conditions. David Katzman (1981) and Elizabeth Clark-Lewis (1983) have illustrated the importance that the shift from live-in to live-out had on improving working conditions. Evelyn Glenn (1986:143) links non-residential jobs to the move towards structuring the occupation to resemble industrialized wage labour: "Work and nonwork life are clearly separated, and the basis for employment is more clearly contractual—that is, the worker sells a given amount of labour time for an agreed-upon wage." Analyzing the work histories of Chicanas in the southwestern U.S., in this chapter I explore the changes they identify in their experiences as private household workers. Life stories about the occupation point to changing work standards, working conditions, and employer—employee relationships. Employer—employer relationships and the structure of housework itself are the two areas in domestic service experiencing change. Although closely related, each area is reviewed and discussed.

Chicana Work Experiences

Life histories of twenty-five Chicanas employed as private household workers in a major southwestern urban region point to various areas in the employer-employee relationship and the structure of paid housework that are undergoing change. Three parts of the narratives that illustrate changes in paid domestic work are explanations about decisions to remain working in or to return to domestic service and employer-employee conflict. The process of change in the occupation is apparent in the women's comparison with work experience in the past and the present. Comparisons reflect the workers' own assessment of change. The work histories of the Chicana domestics whom I interviewed, direct attention to the calculated choices workers make, even when their choices are limited. Explanations about weighing their limited job opportunities and selecting domestic service over other low-paying, low-status jobs stress the possibilities of improving working conditions. These strategies for making the most of their options suggest trends for the future. Unable to find employment offering job security, advancement, or benefits, Chicanas attempt to change the occupation by minimizing control and personalism.

Descriptions of employer—employee conflict is another indication of changing practices in the occupation. Past analyses of domestics' struggles concentrated almost exclusively on interpersonal relationships between domestic workers of colour and their white women employers. The structure of housework is ignored or treated as an extension of the hierarchical relationship between women from different racial backgrounds. However, the relationship is best conceptualized as an employer—employee relationship and an instance of class struggle. Like so many other employer—employee relationships under capitalism, control over the work process is not cooperative. Worker and employer define their interests in opposition and struggle for control. My research on Chicana household workers describes an active struggle for control of the work process. Only by gaining a measure of control can the employees restructure the work to eliminate demeaning and degrading practices. Conflicts arise from such familiar workers' issues as wages, workload, work pace, raises, breaks, and benefits.

Aspects of paid domestic service undergoing change are related to practices identified by historians in their descriptions of the occupation as live-out work.[1] However, there does appear to be a trend towards eliminating tasks that are considered personal in nature or particularly strenuous and dangerous. Accounts also suggest that the common daily rituals and practices of deferential behaviour may be decreasing. In the interviews, private household workers demonstrated an acute awareness of the cultural meaning attached to requests for uniforms, special eating arrangements, or linguistic and spatial deference. They described resistance to labour which involved acting inferior. Redefining the job and the employer—employee relationship emerge as primary concerns. Accounts about finding new employers reveal that household workers actively negotiate informal labour arrangements that include strategies to eliminate the most oppressive aspects of the occupation and strategies to develop instrumental employer—employee relationships aimed at professionalizing the occupation.

Redefining Paid Domestic Work

The critical locus of household workers' struggle to improve conditions is to define the work on the basis of a contract—by the house or apartment—not as hourly work. While informal work arrangements frequently imply a set number of hours, the typical arrangement is referred to as "charging by the house." Mrs. Salazar explains the verbal contract:

When you say you're going to clean a house, after you find out how big it is, you tell them [the employer] "I'll clean it for say sixty dollars." You're not saying how long you're going to be there. To me, that was just a contract between you and the customer and after awhile when you've been there awhile, you know how fast you can work and I was doing it in less than eight hours.

Mrs. Lopez expresses her preference for "charging by the house":

I never liked to work by the hour because if I would work by the hour the lady would just go crazy loading me up with work, with more work and more work to do.

Charging a flat rate also eliminates employers' attempts at speed-up by adding more tasks and forcing the domestic to increase the pace of the work. Glenn (1985) also found that Japanese-American domestics attempt to limit the amount of work by specifying tasks rather than time. Charging a "flat rate" is a significant change in the occupation, particularly in light of the broad range of physical and emotional labour domestics report doing. The list of tasks suggests that many employers purchase labour power rather than labour services; that is, workers are not hired simply to provide the labour service of cleaning the house, but their labour is purchased for a certain amount of hours to do a variety of unspecified tasks. "Charging by the house" involves specifying the tasks and thus, placing boundaries on the job description.

All but one woman interviewed attempted to control the workload and establish a concrete verbal contract outlining the specific tasks. Mrs. Gallegos is the only woman who voiced a different strategy for controlling the amount of tasks given by the employer:

When you work by the hour, they're [employers] not going to line up any work. And once you start using a system, you can do it. . . . take your time, you know. I see a lot of ladies—they [employees] want too much when they [employers] do pay them so much but they [employees] ask too much. I won't go for that. I told them [employers] I work by the hour, I will not take a flat rate cause if it takes me five, six hours, I want to get paid and if it takes four hours that's my problem. I will not work flat rate.

Mrs. Gallegos argues that the hourly wage places a limit on the amount of work and assures the worker that she is paid for all of her labour.

Similar to the dialectic between employer and employee Glenn describes, there is an ongoing negotiation as the domestic attempts to maintain the agreement while the employer attempts to lengthen the working day or to add more tasks. For instance Mrs. Tafoya recalls an incident in which an employer attempted to extract additional unpaid labour:

> I guess the niece came home. I knew the record player was playing and she was kinda—but I thought she was just tapping like you would tap [indicates with her hand on the table], you know. She was dancing and I guess the wax wasn't dry. She made a mess. I said to Mrs. Johnson [employer], I says I'm not going to clean that again. You get your niece to clean that. I did it once and it was beautiful. And I did it because nobody was here and I know that it would dry right. So if you want it redone you have your niece do it. And she says but you're getting paid for it. I says yeah, I got paid for it and I did it.

By refusing to wax the floor over again, Mrs. Tafoya maintained the original labour arrangement.

Mrs. Sanchez gave an account that illustrates her attempt to place limits on the amount of work done and her efforts to maintain the original verbal contract. She described a problem she was having with an employer who was attempting to increase her workload. Mimicking the high-pitched voice of her employer, she repeated the employer's question: "Would you mind doing this? Would you mind doing that?" Mrs. Sanchez confided that she wants to respond by saying, "Yes I do mind and I won't do it," but instead she said, "Well, I'll do it *this* time." She expressed the importance of pointing out to the employer that the task would be done *this* time and not to be expected in the future.

Another strategy Chicanas use to limit the work and reduce employers' efforts to extract unpaid labour involves developing a routine for handling "extras." The women describe preparing a monthly or bimonthly schedule for rotating particular tasks, such as cleaning the stove or refrigerator, and thereby, avoiding many special requests. Another common practice is to establish an understanding with the employer that if one task is added, then one is eliminated. If the employer does not identify the tasks to be eliminated, the employee simply selects one and later explains that there was not enough time for both. Mrs. Garcia recalls learning the strategy from her cousin:

My cousin said, "Do the same thing every time you come in, as far as changing the sheets, vacuum and dust, and window sills, pictures on the walls, and stuff like that unless they ask you to do something extra. Then, maybe don't clean the tile in the bathroom, or just do the windows that really need it, so you can have some time to do this other stuff that they wanted you to do extra." And she said, "Never do more than what they ask you to do, because if you do then you're not really getting paid for it."

Negotiating specific tasks rather than hours also involved defining a routine set of housework tasks and eliminating personal services such as babysitting, laundry, or ironing. Older Chicanas recalled babysitting, ironing, cooking, and doing laundry, but in recent years they rarely do such tasks. Even younger Chicanas in their thirties, some with twelve years experience, only do ironing or laundry for employers they started with ten years ago. Cooking Mexican food was also a task that Chicana household workers avoided. Their reasons for refusing the request suggests that they make a division between paid tasks and a "work of love" and take precautions against selling their personhood:

I only cook for my family.

I didn't want to share my culture with them [employers].

The division of tasks was also apparent in the women's distinctions between the work done by maids and housekeepers or "cleaning ladies." These Chicanas define their work as different from maid's work. Mrs. Montoya's statement illustrates the equation of personal services with maid's work:

I figure I'm not there to be their personal maid. I'm there to do their housecleaning, their upkeep of the house. Most of the women I work for are professionals and so they feel it's not my job to run around behind them. Just to keep their house maintenance clean and that's all they ask.

Another aspect of domestic service the women tried to redefine was the comparison between homemaking activities women engaged in as wives and mothers and the work completed by private household workers. This was particularly apparent in employers' disregard for minimum wage, raises, social security, healthcare, and vacation. In all but two cases, employment in domestic service was not reported to the IRS and these women express relief that income tax is not filed. Three women expressed concern about social security and urged employers to submit the required paper work. Two of the oldest women interviewed are receiving social security benefits as a result of their long-term employers' concern over their welfare.

One third of the women receive benefits unknown to other domestics or other low-status jobs. Nine Chicanas who have worked for employers over a long period of time report that they receive paid vacations. This usually involves no more than one or two days paid per employer. Christmas bonuses are more common that annual raises. However, nine report annual raises and three of the women increase their wages annually by requesting raises or quitting one employer and raising the cost for new employers.

Redefining Employer-Employee Relationships

In order to structure the work as a meaningful and nondegrading activity, domestics struggle to remove employers from controlling decisions. When employers control the work process, domestics are reduced to unskilled labourers and housecleaning becomes mindless hourly work. Furthermore, domestics strive to eliminate the rituals of deference and the stigma of servitude.

In comparing domestic service to other available work options, all of the women cited the flexible work schedule and autonomy they experienced as private household workers. Most of the women consider the flexible schedule as the major advantage domestic service has over other jobs they had held. For instance, Mrs. Salas stated: "I like it [domestic service] because you can choose your hours." For Mrs. Salas, day-work allows her more freedom to change her work schedule than other jobs. Although Chicanas considered flexibility, autonomy, and independence the advantages that domestic service has over other jobs, these characteristics are not inherent features. Domestics have to negotiate directly with employers to establish a flexible work schedule and autonomy on the job.

Like other women employed as day-workers in domestic service, Chicanas worked for several employers. A different employer every day allowed household workers more independence and reduced the employer's control. In recent years some of the women were cleaning more than one house a day and thus, had two or three employers in one day. This was particularly common among Chicanas employed by employers living in condominiums or apartments. Having numerous employers at one time provides workers with the leeway to quit, because one employer is easily replaced with another without affecting the entire work week.

Chicanas used the job flexibility gained as day-workers employed by several employers to rearrange the work week to fit their personal needs. For instance, many of the older women reduce their work week to three or four days, whereas the younger women who needed more income were more likely to clean two apartments a day and work six days a week. A few women, like Mrs. Lovato, used the flexibility to work as a domestic part-time during times of economic crisis:

> I worked for Coors [brewery] for about three years and I would still do housecleaning, sort of part-time in the morning.

Mrs. Mondragon recalled that her decision to return to domestic service after her youngest child entered school was related to the flexible schedule. She was unable to find another job that allowed her to arrange a work schedule around her child's schoolday. Several working mothers with small children also wanted the flexibility of taking their children to work with them.[2]

Job flexibility was further increased in the informal labour arrangement with employers. During the negotiations with employers, Chicanas established work hours that provided the flexibility that other jobs lacked. Although employers struggled to structure the work, Chicanas were insistent about arranging certain work hours and avoided a specification of hours as a condition of their employment. They tried to establish a flexible schedule that included occasional changes in the length of the working day. The personal arrangements and verbal contracts between employer and employee made it possible to negotiate a half day's work or to skip a day. As Mrs. Garcia, a fifty-four year-old domestic, explains:

> You can change the dates if you can't go a certain day and if you have an appointment, you can go later, and work later, just as long as you get the work done. . . . I try to be there at the same time, but if I don't get there for some reason or another, I don't have to think I'm going to lose my job or something.

Independence and autonomy are other characteristics that Chicanas considered advantages domestic service offered over their past jobs. Mrs. Garcia compared the preference for domestic service over other low-paying, low-status jobs:

> I like being free to do the work the way I like it and I like doing housework. . . . They're [employers] not fussy about having to punch a clock like you do when you're working [at other jobs]

that you have to punch a clock and always have to be worried about being there at the same time and have to think I'm going to lose my job.

Mrs. Rojas continued to work as a domestic after her job in a hospital because of the independence the job offers:

> When you work like in a hospital or something, you're under somebody. They're telling you what to do or this is not right. But housecleaning is different. You're free. You're not under no pressure, especially if you find a person who really trusts you all the way. You have no problems.

In the informal labour arrangement, domestic and employer must verbally negotiate working conditions which include tasks, timing, technique, the length of the working day, and payment. Chicanas establish verbal contracts with employers. When starting with a new employer, the domestic works one day, and if the employer is satisfied with her work, the two agree upon a work schedule and the specific tasks to be accomplished. Mrs. Fernandez bases her decision to stay with a new employer by watching for signs of supervision and monitoring and unreasonable expectations:

> You can tell if they're [employers] going to trust you or not. If they're not overlooking—see, you know—over you all the time. If they start looking or saying, "I don't want this moved or I don't want this done or be careful with this"—well, you know, you can be so careful but there's accidents happen. So if they start being picky I won't stay.

Mrs. Lopez classifies the type of employer by the attitude they expose in the first few minutes of their first encounter:

> I have had ladies that have said, "I know you know what to do so I'll leave it to you," or they pull out their cleaning stuff and tell you, "this is for this and this is for that," and I say, "I know, I've done this before." "Oh, okay, I'll let you do it."

Mrs. Rodriquez describes the ideal situation:

> Once the person learns that you're going to do the job they just totally leave you to your own. It's like it's your own home.

The ideal is similar to informal arrangements Glenn (1985) reports. However, half of the women I interviewed explain the ideal situation is achieved after some supervision and negotiation. Such an experience is alluded to in Mrs. Portillo's explanation of why she left an employer:

> I don't want somebody right behind me telling me what to do. I will not work like that and that's why I didn't stay any longer with this lady.

A domestic's priority in the informal labour arrangement is to negotiate a work structure that provides autonomy and independence. Autonomy on the job is created when the worker is in control over the planning and organization of the housework, as well as the work pace and the method. Gaining autonomy also assures the worker that the parameters of the work are maintained. The ideal situation is the worker structuring the work and removing the employer from direct supervision. Chicana domestics stated their desire for autonomy in the common expression, "being your own boss."

An aspect of eliminating the employer from a supervisory role was establishing the worker as the expert on housework. The Chicanas interviewed consider themselves experts. They are aware of the broad range of knowledge they have acquired from cleaning a variety of homes. This includes the removal of stains on various surfaces, tips for reorganizing the home, and the pros and cons of certain brands of appliances. A common practice that stressed the household workers' expertise was the introduction of labour-saving devices or tactics into employers' homes. Mrs. Garcia's experience in removing stains illustrates the expert advice workers offer employers:

> They [employers] just wipe their stoves and then complain, "This doesn't come off anymore." They never took a SOS pad or a scrub brush to scrub it off. They expect it just to come off because they wiped.... Their kitchen floors would have kool-aid stains or they would have it on the counters, so I would just pour Clorox on it and the Clorox would just bring it right up and they would say "But you'll ruin it!" "No it will be alright." "Are you sure?" I never ruined anything from helping them out.

Mrs. Montoya describes the type of advice some employers requested:

> They'll [employers] ask you how to clean the tile up in the bathroom or they ask me—like one of them even ask me how I

did her bed so nice—the corners—because she couldn't do it, you know, so she asked me how I did it and to teach her how to do the corners in her bed. Some of them even ask me how to change a vacuum bag or how to put a belt in the vacuum because they had never done it before and they happen to use at a time that it broke so they asked me how to fix it. So they'll ask me how to do things like that which are really funny.

Mrs. Cortez's habit of providing cleaning hints points to some employers' willingness to accept the expertise of the domestic:

I cut out pieces of cleaning [information] that tell you how to do this an easy way. . . . I'll take them and paste them on like their pantry doors and I'll put them there and then when they go to open [the pantry door] they say, "Oh, that's a good idea." So then they start doing it that way.

As expert cleaners, the women take responsibility for all decisions regarding the structure of the work process, the pace of the housework, and the selection of work materials. Ideally the domestic enters the employer's home, and decides where to begin, and arranges the appliances and cleaning products accordingly. She paces herself to finish in a certain number of hours. If she needs to leave early, she can speed-up and not take a break; in other cases, a more leisurely pace is indicated. The situation differs from the speed-ups that Glenn (1985:161) describes in her study: "If the worker accomplished the agreed-upon task within the designated period, the employer added more tasks, forcing the worker to do everything faster."

Chicana domestics, not unlike African-American and Japanese-American domestics, did not necessarily find an affective relationship the ingredient for a satisfying working relationship. In fact, the opposite is the case, because affective relationships provide more opportunities for exploitation. Frequently, close friendships result in fictitious kinship references, such as a younger employer adopting the domestic as a surrogate mother. Redefining the work obligation as a "family" obligation places the domestic in a difficult position. As Mrs. Portillo explains, the personal nature of the relationship creates an atmosphere conducive to manipulation: "Some people use their generosity to pressure you." Maintaining the conditions of the contract also becomes difficult because extra requests are made as requests from a friend rather than an employer. When employers use personalism as a means to extract additional labour, many domestics were able to increase their pay by threatening to quit.

However, when they no longer felt in control, many choose to quit and find another employer. Minimizing the contact with employers was the most successful strategy for gaining control over the work process.

Employers are reluctant to turn over the control of the process to the domestic. Instead they attempt to structure the work to be supervised and monitored. Chicanas report that some employers gave detailed instructions on how to clean their home: washing the floor on hands and knees, using newspaper instead of paper towels on the windows, or even which direction to scrub the wall. Mrs. Portillo, a retired domestic with thirty years experience, expresses the frustration of working for an employer who retained control of the work process:

> I used to have one lady that used to work right along with me. I worked with her three years. I found it hard. I was taking orders. I'm not the type to want to take orders. I know what I'm going to do. I know what general housecleaning is.

Under supervised conditions, domestics find themselves simply taking orders, which reduces their work activity to quick, monotonous gestures.

Mrs. Sanchez voices the general consensus that the least interaction with employers, the better the working conditions: "The conflicts have been mostly with people who stay at home and really just demand the impossible." Five domestics even commented that they selected employers on the basis of whether the employer worked outside the home.

Chicanas argue that employed women are more appreciative of the housework done and are relieved to turn over the planning and execution of cleaning to the domestic. Unemployed women, on the other hand, are portrayed as "picky" and unwilling to relinquish control. Three domestics I interviewed suggest that unemployed women feel guilty because they are not doing the work themselves and thus, retain control and responsibility for the housework. Mrs. Lucero's description represents the distinctions domestics make between women who work outside the home and fulltime homemakers:

> I think women that weren't working were the ones that always had something to complain about. The ones that did work were always satisfied. I've never come across a lady that works that has not been satisfied. Those that are home and have the time to do it themselves, and don't want to do it, they are the ones that are always complaining, you know, not satisfied, they always want more and more. You can't really satisfy them.

Employed women tend to be ideal employers because they are rarely home and are unable to supervise.

The selection of employers is essential in maximizing the advantages domestic service has over other available jobs. Four characteristics that the women most frequently mention as qualities of a "good" employer are trust, respect, the understanding that family responsibilities come before work, and the ability to maintain a system for housecleaning. Only those employers who trust their employees will allow the worker to structure the housework. Respect indicates that employers are not trying to affirm and enhance their status by establishing the domestic's inferior status. Most of the women felt that family obligations, such as a sick child, superseded the work obligation. Therefore, they sought employers willing to accommodate occasional changes in the schedule. Domestics prefer to work for employers who maintain the house between cleanings and are not "dirty." "Bad" employers are characterized as "constantly looking over their shoulder," expecting the domestic to pick up after the children, leaving too many notes, and adding extra tasks. Domestics control their work environment to a large degree by replacing undesirable employers with more compatible ones.

The importance of redefining social relationships in domestic service is most apparent in the women's distinctions between the work they do and maid's work. Mrs. Fernandez, a thirty-five-year-old domestic, indicates the distinction in the following account:

> They [the employer's children] started to introduce me to their friends as their maid. "This is our maid, Angela." I would say, "I'm not your maid. I've come to clean your house and a maid is someone who takes care of you and lives here or comes in everyday and I come once a week and it is to take care of what you have messed up. I'm not your maid. I'm your housekeeper."

Mrs. Rojas, a thirty-three-year-old domestic with twelve years of experience, equates deferential behavior to being a maid:

> One or two [employers] that I work for now have children that are snotty, you know, they thought that I was their maid, or they would treat me like a maid, you know, instead of a cleaning lady.

Chicanas attempted to enforce a new set of norms that transform the domestic–mistress relationship to a customer–vender relationship. In their struggle to change the occupation, the Chicanas altered the employer's role to client or customer. This new definition of the relationship lessened the opportunity for psychological exploitation and fostered the elimination of personal services. The workers' struggle against the personalization of the employer–employee relationship involves a struggle against the personalization of the work.

In order to convince employers to accept the new working relationship, private household workers have to present the advantages. One strategy used to convince an employer not to be a supervisor is to create a situation for the employer that demands more detailed supervision. This includes such tactics as doing only the tasks requested and nothing else, not bothering to inform the employer that the worker used the last vacuum bag or used up the cleaning materials, and refusing to offer the employer assistance in fixing a simple mechanical problem in an appliance. Consequently, employers who refuse to shift control and responsibility are confronted with domestics who take no interest in or responsibility for completing the housework.

To redefine their work as skilled labour, Chicanas capitalize on the fact that employed women are no longer interested in supervising the work of the private household worker. Women hiring domestics to escape the double-day syndrome cannot reap the benefits of the work if they supervise the work of a "menial labourer." Acknowledging housework as skilled labour affirms the worth of the housewives' housework. In shifting housecleaning to "expert housekeepers" the housewife fulfills her responsibility to the family by obtaining skilled services; and in doing so, she defines the work as difficult, time consuming, and requiring skilled labour.

Discussion

The research on Chicana household workers supports many of the findings on working conditions found in studies on women of colour in domestic service. Employers maintain a benevolent attitude towards "their" domestics, demanding loyalty and deference. Employers treat employees with the type of kindness reserved for domestic animals or pets and children, or at times even "nonpersons." Even with the change to hourly work, the employer–employee relationship retains characteristics of the mistress–maid or master–servant relationship. However, my findings also suggest a broader range of relationships co-existing in the occupation.

Other researchers have centred their analysis on the interpersonal relationship between the domestic and employer rather than the work process. An overview of their findings illustrates that workers attempt to control the work structure. Dill (1979) and Tucker (1988) discussed a strategy that domestics use to control wages and benefits by carefully selecting wealthy employers. Dill referred to the strategy as "building a career," explaining that domestics find wealthy employers who can provide high wages and benefits that increase the domestic's social position and feelings of self worth. Coley (1981) noted a similar technique among unionized members who created upward mobility for themselves by assessing the occupational structure and selecting the job description that conferred more money and status.

The increased autonomy, independence, pay, and benefits can be attributed to the different circumstances each faced in the labour market. Unlike many of the Black domestics studied in the Eastern U.S., this group of Chicanas were not sole supporters of the family, nor union members; and unlike the Japanese-American women in Glenn's (1985) study, most of the Chicanas were second or third generation and were much younger. The Chicanas whom I interviewed have more formal education, and for the most part are not being replaced by newly arrived immigrants.[3]

In some areas of the United States, a seller's market makes it possible for domestic workers to demand more money and autonomy. The shift to day-work has provided new alternatives in the occupation. Increasing numbers of middle-class women hire a private household worker on a schedule—once a week or even every other week. Many domestics employed as day-workers have regular systems for maintaining a number of employers. Workers are thus able to replace employers with more ease than they could previously and this increases their autonomy.

Nevertheless, domestic service remains in the informal sector of the economy, and the number of undocumented workers employed as domestics is expanding. In the late twentieth century both minimum wage and social security legislation were extended to cover most types of domestic work, but many employers fail to comply and many employees prefer to work "off the record." Even though organizations such as the National Committee on Household Employment (NCHE) in the U.S. have enjoyed some success in publicizing the plight of household workers, unionization efforts have not yet had a demonstrative effect upon the occupation. For most domestics the occupation continues to be regulated by community norms and values determining informal labour arrangements made between the private household worker and her employer. Alejandro Portes's (1983:157) definition of the informal sector describes the current condition in domestic service:

> It is work that is unstandardized, and unorganized, requires no formal training, and from which employees may be fired for lack of cause. Its workers are not included in the protective legislation

covering wages, illness, accidents or retirement. And its labour is far more "elastic"; hired in good times and discharged during bad; hired for unspecified periods and fired without notice.

Acknowledgement

Chapter two, by Mary Romero, is part of a recently published book: *Maid in the USA*, N.Y. Routledge, 1992. The research was funded by a grant from the Business and Professional Women's Foundation and a University of California President's Fellowship.

Notes

1. In her study of the transition from live-in to day-work among African-American women in Washington D.C., Elizabeth Clark-Lewis (1985:21) captured the significance of the change to day-work: "The women saw the change as a step toward autonomy and independence, and away from the dependency and indignity of live-in work. It was the difference between a 'job,' or 'work,' and 'serving.'" Day-workers were able to replace employers at less personal cost and could afford to be less tolerant of poor working conditions, importunate employers, and low pay. The shift to day-work gave workers more autonomy because they could have several employers at one time (Katzman 1981; Glenn 1985).

2. Interviewees in Tucker's study discuss taking their children to jobs (1988:119-152). This is also a practice cited in Ximena Bunster and Elsa M. Chaney (1985:141). They found that some of the live-out maids with preschool children took the children to work.

3. At the time of the study, Mexican immigrants were not perceived as competition; however, Chicanas indicated they were incorporating Mexican women into their networks and urged them not to lower standards. However, several women expressed concern over Vietnamese immigrants' willingness to work for less pay as well as to include gardening along with household chores. For the most part, Chicanas operated a domestic's market and, therefore, used the latitude to select employers who showed respect and professional behaviour.

CHAPTER THREE

CARING FOR THE CHILDREN

Jane Bertrand

Editors' Note

T his chapter is based on one of five papers that were written to provide a substantive framework for a national childcare conference co-sponsored by the Canadian Day Care Advocacy Association and the Ontario Coalition for Better Child Care in October 1992. *Putting the Pieces Together: A Child Care Agenda for the 1990s* is a forthcoming collection of these papers. Thus research for this chapter is principally derived from policy documents and their critiques, as well as the activist politics of the childcare movement. Unlike the other areas of paid domestic work described in this book, there is a dearth of qualitative research involving interviews and life history approaches to the study of childcare workers. We know little about the issues of class, race, and ethnicity concerning these workers, nor about the social relations of their workplaces and their households. And yet the care of children is one of the most basic forms of both unpaid and paid domestic labour.

Most of the research to date has focussed on the quality of childcare rather than the working conditions and lives of the workers themselves. This may be related to the fact that much of the organizing and activism around childcare has been by parents, whose main interest has been their children. The lives of childcare workers have often been treated as of secondary importance, and thus these workers have become at least partially invisible. By indicating some of the contradictions between the requirements of quality childcare (among them the need to avoid high labour turnover) and the difficulty of meeting these requirements through low-paid labour, this chapter lays important groundwork and points to some future research directions.

Introduction

More than sixty thousand people now care for young children in regulated childcare across Canada. These workers are an important component of an emerging Canadian childcare system that is staffed predominantly by female workers and is often viewed as an extension of women's traditional roles as mothers and homemakers. This childcare system has yet to develop clearly understood rules and norms for its paid workers. Because this is a recent phenomenon, very few childcare staff themselves have had personal early childhood experiences in licensed childcare and education settings. They bring their own childhood experiences and perhaps parenting experiences, first school experiences (often kindergarten), and (if young enough) a "Sesame Street" approach to help define and understand childcare settings and the role of staff in these settings. However, as this chapter demonstrates, the large numbers of childcare staff with a post-secondary education and further training in early childhood education programs challenges notions of childcare work as "unskilled" and therefore readily devalued labour.

Regulated childcare settings are diverse and include licensed childcare centres and nursery schools, regulated family home childcare, parent— child resource centres, kindergarten programs, and out-of-school programs. Childcare employers may be small community-based boards of directors, non-profit multi-service agencies, community colleges, municipalities, school boards, or private individuals or companies. The range of settings and the age groups and numbers of children served have grown significantly over the past decade. As well, each province and territory in Canada has established its own legislation and regulations for licensed childcare settings. Childcare policies and services vary across the country, creating a patchwork quilt of more differences than similarities (Goelman 1992).

There are no set role titles for workers: manager, director, coordinator, supervisor, and administrator are all terms that may be used for the person "in charge." Teacher, childcare worker, daycare worker, program staff, caregiver, and early childhood educator are used to describe the people who directly plan and carry out children's daily care and activities. In part, these differences in terms reflect provincial and territorial variation, but they also reflect different views of the "care" and "education" functions of childcare centres.

As in other traditional female job sectors, salaries are lower than in male-dominated sectors requiring comparable education and training. Also typical of female job sectors, only 20 percent of childcare staff in Canada are represented by a collective bargaining unit, compared to 30 percent in the general labour force (Karyo Communications 1992). Low salaries in childcare reflect the notion that nurturing young children is an inherent part of a woman's role. The primary reward is assumed to be the satisfaction involved in fulfilling this role. Monetary compensation has been considered a secondary, less important reward. Also, the care of young children has been an invisible part of the economy. Typically, mothers who are full-time homemakers have fulfilled the role without financial reward. Therefore, most early childcare has been considered "free."

The data that is presented in this chapter on salaries, benefits, and working conditions should be considered in light of the fact that staff working in Canadian childcare centres are ninety-eight percent female, forty-one percent with children living at home and almost ninety percent of childbearing age (Karyo Communications 1992). These are women who presently have childcare needs of their own or are likely to have such responsibilities in the near future. An inherent contradiction is that while they care for other people's children, their own childcare and other personal needs may be neglected due to low salaries, and lack of benefits and job protection.

Throughout this century, early childhood education professional organizations in Canada and the United States have focused primarily on the quality of the environments made available to children. Efforts to improve significantly staff economic circumstances have not been emphasized (Finkelstein 1988).

This approach to professionalism is more typical of female-dominated sectors than of male-dominated sectors, such as medicine, law and, engineering, where working conditions, benefits, and financial remuneration have been primary concerns. However, even female-dominated sectors, such as elementary school teaching and nursing, which historically began with an emphasis on the quality of services provided, also developed effective collective bargaining structures that have promoted reasonable remuneration and benefits and protected other goals of professionalism. The different value accorded the work of teachers in schools versus that of childcare workers may be partly attributed to corporate interest in educating those who are perceived as future workers, whereas infants and young children are presently less likely to be considered in this light.

This chapter explores the common characteristics of childcare staff, whose roles and responsibilities are often ambiguous, reflecting the changing range of services in the childcare sector. It considers how workers are organized in regulated childcare settings by examining staff salaries, benefits, and working conditions. The chapter discusses the future of childcare workers, their place in a Canadian national childcare policy, and the roles and responsibilities of provincial and territorial governments, professional organizations, unions, and post-secondary educational institutions.

Childcare Staff: A Key to High Quality Childcare

A review of research studies conducted over the past ten years in Canada, the United States, England, Western Europe, Bermuda, and New Zealand concludes that childcare staff are critical determinants of quality in early childcare and education programs (Doherty 1991). Several of the studies indicate that the amount and quality of interaction between children and staff is the most important factor for positive child outcomes in centre- or home-based childcare settings.

The quality of child–staff interactions is determined by a number of factors, including the amount and type of training, staff–child ratios, group size, program size, staff turnover rate, and job satisfaction. Several details are known from the research:

* Working with young children requires skills and knowledge that are provided through formal education and training programs. The current research demonstrates a strong relationship between program quality, staff education, training in child development, and early childhood education practices (Whitebook et al. 1990).
* Low staff turnover promotes program stability for children and their families through the development of consistent relationships. High staff turnover has quite a different effect, creating a lack of consistency and instability.
* Child development experts believe that optimal staff–child ratios are:
  Infants (0 - 18 months)   1:3
  Toddlers (18 - 30 months)   1:4
  Preschool (30 months - 5 years)   1:6
  Kindergarten (4 and 5 years)   1:8
  School-age (6 - 9 years)   1:10
  (National Association for the Education of the Young Child 1990; Harms 1980; Doherty 1991). These ratios allow for frequent interactions between children and adults and individualized attention for each child.
* Job satisfaction is determined by a number of work environment variables, including salary levels, amount of time for preparation work, staff–child ratio, and the program's administration style (Doherty 1991).

Other factors related to positive child–staff interactions are linked to specific contextual factors: regulatory environment (legislation, licensing, monitoring, and enforcement), auspices (non-profit, municipal, or commercial), and funding (Doherty 1991). An American study found that auspice was the strongest predictor of quality. Commercial childcare centres were related to lower quality care (Whitebook et al. 1990).

Working Conditions

A study of childcare staff in the U.S. found that staff wages were an important predictor of quality childcare. The study also found that the rate of staff turnover is related to salary, benefits, working conditions, and employment practices (Whitebook et al. 1990). However, results of a recent national Canadian survey indicate that staff in regulated childcare settings are poorly compensated for their training. Wages have not kept pace with inflation and fall near the bottom of industrial wage rates. The majority of staff receive few benefits beyond legislated requirements. Poor working conditions are reported as a source of considerable frustration for workers (Karyo Communications 1992). Recent studies indicate only a third of staff are entitled to paid preparation time or paid release time for professional development. Less than half had written job descriptions and only a quarter had written personnel policies or written contracts (Schom-Moffat 1986; Karyo Communications 1992; Doherty 1991).

This section highlights the situation of staff in regulated childcare centres. Little recent information about the wages and working conditions of regulated home childcare providers has been collected for Canada as a whole.

Salaries

In 1984, the first Canadian survey on childcare salaries and working conditions was carried out. That study, *The Bottom Line: Wages and Working Conditions of Childcare Employees* found the average childcare wage across all positions was $7.29 per hour. The most recent survey, in 1991, found that the average wage had risen to $9.60 per hour. Adjusted for inflation, the 1984 average wage would now be $10.05 per hour, indicating a 45 percent drop in the *real* wages of childcare staff over the past seven years (Karyo Communications 1992).

The 1991 survey also found that wages for childcare staff varied in relationship to the centre's auspice or sponsorship. Staff working in municipal childcare centres were likely to be paid the highest wages, while staff employed in commercial centres were paid the lowest wages. Prince Edward Island, where commercial centres reported the highest salaries, was the only province or territory to vary from this norm. The study reported that overall staff in non-profit centres in Canada earned 25 percent more than staff in commercial centres across all staff positions. Childcare staff ranked better salaries as the single most important improvement to increase job satisfaction and reduce staff turnover rates. Unionized staff earn, on average, 33 percent higher wages than non-unionized staff (Karyo Communications 1992). However, as mentioned earlier, the unionization of childcare staff is low compared to other sectors of the labour force.

A number of factors contribute to a low union membership rate. Childcare centres are usually small workplaces, individually operated by community boards of directors or individual owners, and unions are reluctant to organize small bargaining units where contract negotiations are expensive and time-consuming. Workers tend to have close relationships with their employers (often parents using the childcare centre) and view unionization as confrontational. Also they have often seen (or perhaps been encouraged to see) a contradiction between seeking appropriate economic rewards and supporting early childhood education as a profession (Griffen 1989).

Benefits

Work-related benefits are important factors contributing to the long-term value of a job and security for staff. Pensions and disability insurance are necessary for women to achieve a more equitable financial position in Canadian society. Yet recent studies indicate that less than a quarter of childcare staff receive a pension and only slightly more receive long-term disability benefits (Schom-Moffat 1986; Karyo Communications 1992).

Except for workers in municipal centres, most workers received few job benefits. Such benefits as were provided varied considerably according to auspice. Staff in commercial settings received substantially fewer benefits than staff in non-profit centres and far fewer benefits than staff in municipal centres. Reduced childcare fees for parent employees was found to be the only benefit more likely to be offered by commercial centres (Schom-Moffat 1986; Doherty 1992; Karyo Communications 1992). The American national childcare staffing survey found that reduced fees for parent employees was linked to centres offering the poorest quality care (Whitebook et al. 1990).

Training and Education

In Canada staff training requirements in regulated childcare settings are determined through provincial or territorial legislation and regulations. Three jurisdictions (New Brunswick, Yukon, and Northwest Territories) have no formal requirements; Newfoundland requires training only for supervisory staff; and Manitoba requires that two-thirds of the staff must have completed a one- or two-year training program in early childhood education. Nine provinces require completion of an educational training program in early childhood education for at least some staff working in regulated childcare. The length of required training varies from orientation courses of fifty hours to two-year certificate or diploma programs. Many jurisdictions allow work experience or government approval to substitute for required qualifications. However, there are few provincial or territorial training or education requirements for regulated family-home childcare.

Quality staff (staff who promote healthy child development in early childhood settings) are associated with post secondary school education and training in early childhood education (Doherty 1991; Whitebook et al. 1990). The national staff survey reported that seven out of ten staff working in regulated early childhood education settings had a post-secondary credential (certificate, diploma, or university degree in some area of study). Forty percent of the staff surveyed had either a one-year or two-year early childhood education diploma or certificate. Almost five percent reported a bachelor's degree in early childhood education (Karyo Communications 1992).

The academic and field-practice components of early childhood education training programs are based on the knowledge, skills, and attitudes presumed to be important in preparing people to work effectively with young children in a variety of settings. A recent review of early childhood training programs across Canada found many similarities. The majority of programs reviewed included content in child development, programming, communication, family studies, assessment and observation, health, safety and nutrition, special needs, and history of early childhood education (Norpark 1991).

Over the past twenty years there has been considerable pressure on early childhood education training programs to meet the expanding and diversified needs of regulated childcare settings. Most training programs were geared initially to train nursery school teachers who would work with preschool children in half-day programs. Today, the same one- or two-year programs are expected to prepare individuals to work with children from infancy to ten or twelve years in a variety of fulltime and part-time settings. There is growing recognition that childcare programs must recognize and respect linguistic, cultural, and racial differences. Also there must be equitable childcare opportunities for children with special needs. A report on Native childcare (Seto-Thomas 1990) emphasizes the importance of culturally appropriate childcare programs for Native communities.

Future Directions

Childcare operations are based on fee-for-service, with staff costs accounting for 75 to 90 percent of a program's budget. Herein lies the contradiction between quality programming and affordability. Any improvement to salaries brings an increase in parent fees. There is also a relationship here between the entrance of women (who are traditionally unpaid childcare workers in the home) into paid work and a concurrent need for childcare, while childcare workers, who are mostly women, bear the burden of low salaries.

In many provinces, small direct grants are available to regulated programs. However, this funding is not enough to significantly alter the low salary and benefit scenario. There must be a shift to public funding of childcare programs. Parents could still be asked to make a contribution based on family income but increased public funds would ensure basic costs were met. Ontario is one jurisdiction which has taken steps to introduce pay equity legislation covering childcare workers but the legislation is inadequate, largely because it does not stipulate that pay equity for this sector must be achieved within a reasonable time frame. However the proposed legislation does extend coverage to female workplaces and provides 100 percent public funding to address wage inequities.

Early childhood education training programs should be designed to create opportunities for further education and career options. The historical split between education and childcare is artificial and ineffective. As the childcare and education sectors coordinate and sometimes begin to merge programs for children and families, the training programs must also be coordinated. Training programs for grade school teachers and childcare staff should work together to build a common base so individuals may more easily move back and forth between education and childcare programs. A common training base will also bring childcare and school programs closer together.

In conclusion, in spite of minimal qualification requirements across the country and consistently low salaries, 70 percent of childcare workers had some post-secondary credentials and 40 percent had specific training in early childhood education (Karyo Communications 1992). There is also interest in all parts of Canada among childcare workers for further educational opportunities. The growing evidence supporting the link between trained staff and healthy child development outcomes should persuade governments and parents that a custodial solution to childcare is not a good solution.

In Canada, over the last two decades, childcare activists, feminist women's groups, unions, and progressive social service and policy organizations have worked together to advocate for childcare services, developing a childcare agenda based on the four principles of universal accessibility, public funding, and comprehensive and high quality care. Early childhood educating professional organizations are becoming more supportive to this childcare agenda and its related campaign for improved working conditions for childcare staff.

Childcare staff have participated in this push to put childcare on the public agenda in Canada. At local, provincial, territorial, and national forums, childcare staff have shown leadership and tenacity in advocating for changes in childcare services. New funding mechanisms which acknowledge reasonable levels of remuneration for childcare staff must be implemented. This will require sustained political activity and a widening coalition of supporters. Qualifications for staff working in childcare programs should be consistent with the best available child development knowledge and reflect the diversity of the children and their families who use childcare services. Together, childcare advocates can explore the role of unions, professional organizations, and educational institutions. Perhaps then new structures can emerge that will strengthen the position of all staff working in childcare settings and ensure quality services for young children.

Acknowledgement

Chapter three is based on a paper written for a national childcare conference co-sponsored by the Canadian Day Care Advocacy Association and the Ontario Coalition for Better Child Care in October 1992 and a publication entitled: *Putting the Pieces Together: A Child Care Agenda for the 1990s.*

CHAPTER FOUR

PUBLIC HOMES: SUBCONTRACTING AND THE EXPERIENCE OF CLEANING

Rusty Neal

Subcontracting is part of an expanding global privatization strategy that over time results in the ownership of companies becoming more concentrated, competition being minimized, and costs escalating, as the quality of working conditions and pay decline. The consolidation of Canadian cleaning companies in Toronto during the 1980s occurred at the same time as increased numbers of international service corporations entered the Canadian labour market.[1] This chapter will discuss how subcontracting has contributed to the expansion and privatization of paid domestic work into the market economy.

Subcontracting is an important structural aspect of the gendered organization of the low-waged, interior-office-cleaning industry that hinders the possibility of achieving equality between women and men through the creation of tiered working conditions and the identification of cleaning as an extension of women's domestic labour. It also intersects with, maintains, and creates divisions based on gender, race, ethnicity, class, and sexuality. This buttressing of the sexual division of labour within the labour market can have a devastating impact on women when a strategy of privatization is being actively pursued. It is precisely because large numbers of women work in the service sector in Canada that we can see, through this example of the experiences of women as subcontracted cleaners, how wide-reaching the implications of structural inequalities are.

This chapter is based on the author's study of women's experiences in subcontracted cleaning in two public sector institutions, a university and a post office. The article also benefits from the author's participation in a cleaners' political lobby group, the Committee for Cleaners' Rights (Neal 1988).[2]

Subcontracting in a Competitive and Changing Environment

> The university pays the cleaning company and the cleaning company pays me. We don't know how much the university pays them to have the place cleaned. And they give us [minimum wage] $4.35 an hour. They are making a killing just sending people out there to work. Even if I wanted to I could never find out how much the university paid Clean Co. (Brazilian-born male cleaner, vacuums and shampoos carpets at night, age twenty-two)

In the office-cleaning industry "contracting-out" or "subcontracting" is the practice whereby an employer, usually a building owner, occupant, or manager, enters into a contractual arrangement with another employer, usually a contract-cleaning company, in order to have the first employer's building cleaned. The relationship between the building owners and the cleaners is a subcontracted one, and subcontracted employees usually perform cleaning that could be or was previously performed by the building owner's employees.

Since the 1960s, in the service sector, the most frequently contracted-out services in Canada have included janitorial, cafeteria, and security services. During the 1980s subcontracting was increasingly prevalent in the large buildings owned by corporate entities in the growing metropolis of multicultural Toronto. During this time contract-cleaning prices per square foot were highly competitive. While prices for contract cleaning were generally not advertised, from 1984 to 1986 the costs of cleaning services for office buildings declined significantly, with one large contractor moving from $1.15 per square foot to $0.85.[3] At that time, a study by the Institute of Real Estate Management of the [American] National Association of Realtors surveyed their membership and estimated that payroll costs for cleaners represented less than 10 percent of the average operating costs of downtown office buildings.[4]

Profits for subcontractors, as opposed to those building owners who directly employ workers, are built on the relatively lower wages of subcontracted employees. The cost advantage of low wages is at the expense of workers' incomes, working conditions, and the actual maintenance of the building. The recruitment of so-called "marginal workers" into the office-cleaning industry is necessary to maintain low wages and counter resistance to the attendant conditions. Over two hundred private-contract companies vie for these workers, using a variety of recruitment techniques based on newspaper notices and social-cultural networking.

The "cost advantage" for subcontractors is accomplished throughout the industry by cutting wages, eliminating benefits, reducing the labour force, eliminating overtime payments whenever possible, changing administrative and accounting procedures, and minimizing equipment, training, and supervision expenses. Subcontracting costs include a profit margin for subcontractors that is not necessary when cleaners are directly employed. However, a loss of management of the delivery process often results in deteriorating services (Bernstein 1986), and in-house maintenance services are frequently required to correct problems created by the subcontracting relationship. As well, extra costs not specified in contracts and overcharging due to auditing problems often occur.

A strike at the post office where this research was conducted raises questions about the "cost advantage" of subcontracting. During the strike, Canada Post was able to pay replacement workers higher rates than the striking subcontracted cleaners had been paid. The post office also hired thirty extra security guards and several photographers and authorized unlimited overtime pay for management and security personnel. This added expense went toward supporting an anti-union, private contract-cleaning company rather than toward an increase in cleaners' wages and an improvement in their working conditions.

The common practice of "ghosting"[5] by contractors in the 1980s in Toronto intensified cleaners' tasks and meant that more work had to be completed in less time, or left undone. At the post office the extraction of contract money that was routed directly to the contractor via "ghost" employees was one of the many issues that sparked cleaners' anger and encouraged them, with union support, to strike in 1987/88.

At the Toronto School Board, contracting out cleaning services has been a practice since the 1970s. Fortunately the poor performance of contracting cleaning companies in the Metro Toronto Roman Catholic Separate School Board and the implementation of a clause in the current cleaners' collective agreement are delaying the contracting-out of cleaning services (Ross and Calvert 1988).

In neither the university nor the post office sites that were studied, did subcontracting result in more efficient or controlled cleaning (as is sometimes argued in building management trade magazines), in spite of cleaners' efforts to do the best job they could. Likewise, a British study of cleaning services in the early 1980s in the U.K. demonstrates that the quality of cleaning services in the public sector rapidly deteriorates when the services are contracted out (Hanrahan 1983 cited in Paul 1984).

Subcontracting and Successor Rights as Feminist Issues

The [cleaning] industry, which works on contracts is exempt from "successor rights" clauses in Ontario legislation. That means the workers can be fired when the contract changes hands. Without a union and a collective agreement, cleaners as a group are vulnerable to super-exploitation by the industry. Postal cleaners have decided to organize and fight for their rights. (Canadian Union of Postal Workers 1987, pamphlet from a legal strike that began in January 1987 after twelve months of negotiations)

Economic structures in Canada have historically depended on a gendered division of labour.[6] However, today, with over 80 percent of all employed women in Canada working in the service sector (Canada 1990), employment practices in that sector are of considerable consequence for women. The cause of cleaners was first taken up in 1975 by the Ontario Advisory Committee on the Status of Women, on behalf of cleaners at Modern Building Cleaners, who were losing their jobs because of the subcontracting policies of the Ontario Ministry of Government Services. More recently, in the cleaners' strikes of the late 1980s, the rights and working conditions of women service workers, including cleaners, have been recognized and supported as part of the larger struggle for fair and just employment in a time of economic restructuring.

As the National Action Committee on the Status of Women (1991) publicly argues, all women's issues, including racism and poverty, are aspects of structural inequities and economic restructuring. Subcontracting in industries such as cleaning has a disproportionate impact on women and is one aspect of a larger strategy of privatization on the part of both industry and government in the 1990s. The research on which this chapter is based indicates that practices such as subcontracting in cleaning are not just a local form of imposing discipline and control in the workplace, but are holding down wages and maintaining gendered-differential working conditions internationally.[7]

In spite of the Ontario government's rhetoric of equality in the workplace in the 1980s, cleaners in the province have found that their inequality has been maintained and even extended through the social mechanism of subcontracting, which in turn is being reinforced by moves toward privatization. As both federal and provincial governments have increasingly turned to privatization, subcontracting has been codified by labour legislation arbitration rulings (Ontario 1984, 1986). This legislation gives labour rights to some workers, notably male construction workers, but not to (mainly female) office cleaners. When legislated successor rights do not exist, the discontinuity of wages and rights that results when a contract expires or changes hands means that even if cleaners are unionized they are still threatened with losing their collective agreement every time there is a new contract. This situation has made worker organization in the female-dominated service sector very difficult, although not impossible.[8]

The labour legislation and decision-making bodies which govern this situation, though apparently gender neutral, with no mention of men or women in their texts, are clearly not gender neutral in practice. Ontario legislation, for example, is derived from an historically constructed masculinist tradition. Many clauses in the Ontario Labour Relations Act were embedded in male structures of power relations, based on male models of "skilled" craft unions that are not suited to the needs of today's female-dominated "unskilled" service occupations.[9] In the case of cleaners this historic legacy is expressed in the rulings of arbitration boards which, through differential allocation of bargaining rights, create a labour climate more favourable to contract companies than to women service workers. Arms-length contracting forces groups of employees such as cleaners to negotiate with contractors who often cannot commit the owners of large buildings to binding agreements.

One of the effects of the traditional masculinist model of work in the cleaning industry has been a structurally divided, two-tiered system of wages, tasks, and working conditions that divides cleaners who work in the same building. Non-unionized, ethnically divided, subcontracted female office cleaners and male carpet cleaners, under the title of "maintenance workers," work at night performing the specific and often repetitive tasks involved in daily office and carpet cleaning. They are for the most part immigrant workers or children of immigrants. The unionized, directly-employed workers, also called "maintenance workers," do other, better-paid, daytime maintenance work of the building and are inevitably male and less likely to be immigrant workers. Thus, directly-employed workers are pitted against subcontracted workers on the basis of performance and responsibility as well as workplace politics. Unlike nonunionized subcontracted cleaners, unionized directly-employed workers are not likely to lose their collective agreements with a change in contract. Post office cleaners interviewed for the study benefit from being affiliated with a union that early on had a vision of what subcontracting and privatization might mean for all of the post office workers.

Research of university cleaners indicated that women are hired to clean offices while men are hired to clean carpets. Gendered pay differentials, ranging from an hourly wage of $4.35 to $5.50 for women and $4.35 to $9 for men, are justified on the basis of allocated duties. However only women are hired for office cleaning and only men for the carpets. Similarly, at the post office women are hired as "light duty" cleaners at rates of $4.50 an hour while men are hired as "heavy duty" cleaners at rates of $4.65 to $4.80 an hour even though the jobs are virtually the same—with the exception of men shovelling some snow in the winter, but women are expected to do it when men are absent. As one woman said:

> Is there any excuse that they give what they pay? Oh they say a man is a man and a woman is a woman. When women do the cleaning, it is light duty and when men do, it is heavy duty. But doing the same work as women can still be called heavy duty if you are a man. (Yugoslavian-born, female "light duty" cleaner, age forty-five)

At both the post office and university workplaces these divisions are reflective of a trend to structurally devalue the work of women through the use of a light-duty and heavy-duty classification system in the cleaning industry in both Toronto and the rest of the province (Wheeler 1987; Mayes 1987). This trend has not been easily contested, even though there have been a number of very public cleaners' strikes. In the 1986 strike, one of the first items to be traded off for more "substantial gains" in the first contract was the principle of equal pay. In spite of an informal protest among the workers, all men were to continue as "heavy duty" cleaners while women remained "light duty" cleaners.

Subcontractors in both the post office and the university appear to view office cleaning as an activity which comes directly out of the household and thus imbue it with the ideology of a "natural" division of labour which should be exploited rather than treated as a resource that should be adequately compensated. This is especially true in an industry predicated on women responding to the market through the provision of cleaning skills, which are assumed to be developed in the home for the benefit of others. With this framework for devaluing women's work it is not surprising that subcontracting as an employment practice in the cleaning industry as a whole is used to impede the struggle for improved employment conditions for women and to build on and support the maintenance of a divided workforce with differential labour rights.

Commodified Housework and Choosing Workers

> I know that one girl is Canadian but the rest of us is immigrant. Anywhere you go. And in the factory too most is immigrant. In the low-paid factory is immigrant. Immigrant and low pay. . . .

You see we are cleaning. (Indian-born, female "light duty" cleaner, age fifty-nine)

Both the post office and the university cleaning companies that were studied in Toronto demonstrated a preference for non-Canadian-born women cleaners. This unofficial policy seems to be based on the belief that women in general, and in particular women of certain ethnic backgrounds, have special cleaning skills and can transfer these skills, such as attention to detail, from their home to another workplace.

The university and post office cleaners who were interviewed came to Toronto because Canada has actively sought immigrant labour.[10] They exemplify the process by which international migration patterns stream newcomers into jobs dependent upon local markets needs. These workers, who are among the approximately twenty thousand office cleaners in Toronto, come from a large number of countries with varying historical and socio-economic conditions. They share the experience of immigration to a new country and similar work environments in the cleaning industries. But many of the cleaners, especially in the post office, are divided in terms of language and culture, creating difficulties in communication among cleaners and between cleaners and their employers.

The contract-cleaning companies rely on the supposed ignorance of these workers concerning Canadian employment and labour practices and their vulnerability as immigrants and as women. Immigrant workers are also more likely to be intimidated when organizing than Canadian workers for a number of reasons: difficulties with the English language, tenuous immigration status, especially if they are refugees or illegal immigrants, past histories that may have been marked by brutal state and worker interactions, and uncertainties in culturally understanding and finding the appropriate avenues for support and redress in the case of company harassment.

Companies therefore are willing, with impunity, to maintain working conditions that would not be tolerated by many Canadian-born cleaners. In the case of the post office, workers were contracted out with a dramatic decrease in wages from $10 an hour as directly-employed workers to $4.50 an hour as subcontracted workers. As a result, and despite labour disruptions, the post office has proceeded with using the practice of subcontracting with other groups of workers, including closing urban and rural post offices and reopening privatized ones.

Not all companies demonstrate a preference for immigrant workers. Those located outside of Toronto lack access to a large immigrant labour force. In small town Ontario for instance it is young women and older women who are still preferred as cleaners. Regardless of geographical location, gender is the most important factor in the choice of workers for subcontracted cleaning:

> Cleaners' rights are absolutely a women's issue, not just because cleaners are mostly women, but because cleaning is [seen as] traditionally women's work, and because few people ever see these people at work, it's neglected and trivialized and gets no respect. (Judy Darcy as co-chair of the Committee for Cleaner's Rights)

Many cleaners understand the ideology behind the social relations and one Portuguese woman explained her own participation in paid cleaning work as being related to the fact that it was the same as housework:

> I know it's important. Can you imagine if I didn't clean? But nobody really knows what we do, but it's like housework in some ways. It's boring, I clean. It's like housework, you don't really see the results and if you know how to move your hands you can do it. . . . You don't have to have anything, as long as you know how to do housework, this is the same, the same kind of work. And we girls know how to do both. My brothers and father do nothing. (Portuguese-born, female night cleaner, shares her cleaning jobs with her sister, age eighteen)

Whether the multitasked work of housework is actually the same kind of work as routinized office cleaning makes little difference to its definition as women's work. What matters more than the actual tasks is the creation of the ideology of cleaning as women's service work and the notion of the appropriateness of this sexual division of labour. Because women are assumed to know how to clean there is little perceived need for training on the employers' part and little opportunity for advancement. What opportunity does exist for higher wages is attached to the ability to operate cleaning machines. These machines however are most often reserved for men. Some male workers will not show women how to use leverage in the operation of heavy machines, thereby confirming their own sense of superiority through physical strength.

Responsibilities in the home and the patriarchal structure of authority under which some of the women live also mean that women often have different burdens of responsibility than their male counterparts. Many of the women who cleaned at the university have younger children with them while they work. They also have a different kind of work at home than the men, some of it similar to the work they have just completed at the office building. While women often contest the division of labour in the workplace, Livingstone and Luxton (1989) suggest that working-class women are also contesting male privilege as it is experienced in the gendered division of labour in the home. Some men are responding by assuming more responsibilities in the home. However, this is a recent trend and the redistribution of domestic labour is minimal or nonexistent in the worlds of many of the post office and university cleaners that I interviewed. In both the university and the post office the notion of extending women's work from the home into the market is invoked by contract companies to keep women's work gendered.

The Daily Work of Office Cleaning: A Description
However diverse their previous experiences, women cleaners have the common experience of being low-paid, "unskilled" workers. Most work with metal carts loaded with cleaning equipment, rags, dusters, dustpans, various cleaning chemicals, Windex, garbage bags, sometimes mops and brooms, and always a pail of soapy water. Cleaners clean and empty garbage pails and ashtrays in offices, meeting rooms, classrooms (the university), mail sorting rooms, and rest rooms (the post office); gather garbage and deposit it in large bags at the elevators (the university) or take it to be collected for the compactor (the post office). They clean and dust desk tops, phones, and tables, push in chairs, and pick up and discard litter and paper. In washrooms, they clean the toilet bowls, urinals, mirrors, sinks, and sanitary receptacles; empty garbage containers and change toilet paper rolls and hand towels; fill soap dispensers, wipe, wash, and shine walls and doors. They also turn off machines, check locked doors, and attend to various small details of order. Many provide extra personal services by watering plants and passing messages.

Women wheel their carts, which get heavier as garbage is loaded onto them, wherever they go. Although these carts are necessary for the women's work they are not always kept in repair by the cleaning companies because of the need to keep costs down. As a result, toes and feet are often banged, bruised, and sometimes broken, especially when building security guards (who work for a different contract company) turn out the lights to a given area without any notice to the cleaners. The daily grind of bending, lifting, stooping, pushing, and pulling takes its toll on many workers, especially older and elderly women.[11] Swollen ankles, sore backs and arms, and bruises from falls are common ailments for cleaners. Breathing the cigarette ashes as they fly about from trays and the effects of allergies to soaps and detergents are recurrent problems unless cleaners devise their own personal systems for covering ashes and buy their own gloves.

Subcontracted companies do little to respond to any of the suggestions made by cleaners to improve work organization for health or safety reasons. Language differences and a refusal to operate in more than one language also exacerbates health and safety conditions. A number of cleaners, for instance, regularly experienced chemical spills when using toilet cleaners, which in the case of the university, are distributed in small unlabelled containers as a means of saving money. When chemicals are labelled at the post office they are labelled in English only and are not translated into the various languages of the workers or into WHMIS symbols.[12] As a result cleaners are often unaware of the strength of the chemicals until their first accident.

In addition to confronting the health and safety hazards mentioned above, women cleaners also confront degrading and sometimes threatening graphics and texts in the bathrooms that they clean, as well as sexual harassment and assault from building occupants and co-workers. In the men's bathrooms that they clean, they are daily reminded of their subordinate position in the workplace:

> The women's washrooms don't bother me so much because its mostly women's lib stuff and poetry. But I hate the men's washrooms. The graffiti is always sexual, rude, and unpleasant. (Canadian-born, female nighttime office cleaner, age twenty-four)

Defaced with graphic texts and illustrations, the men's washrooms at the university remind cleaners that they are sexual objects in the eyes of men, although for self protection many women try to adopt the attitude of, "I clean it, I don't see it." University washroom graffiti is often very sexually explicit and derogatory to women and interpreted by the cleaners as directed specifically to them as the women who clean the stalls and walls. Due to the sensitivity of the "forelady" (the company term for a female supervisor), women cleaners in the university are able to refuse to clean men's washrooms when the walls become intolerable for them. However it will still be a woman, the "forelady," who is required to clean them.

At the post office, where entrance to the building is much more tightly regulated and male cleaners clean men's washrooms, the graffiti is much less explicit than at the university. This gives some credence to the argument that even though the vast majority of men think very little about the washroom graffiti that they read and see on a regular basis, at least some of the men at the university may write/draw the demeaning words and images realizing that it is women, and often women whom they can identify, who clean the walls.

Unlike men who work as cleaners, women cleaners are often harassed by building occupants. At the university men may enter from the streets, easily bypassing the rather lax security presence in the university, both when the library is open to the public and when it is not. For cleaners, both at the university and the post office, working in isolation makes them easy targets for harassment and assault, especially by men at night, and women were aware of this.

Several women who worked at the university described being stopped in the halls by men they were trying to avoid. One was repeatedly photographed against her will by one of the male students, while another was continually followed by a man whom she feared:

> It's just the way they look at you it just make you think.... .They kinda come near to you and I hate that and I walk back and they keep walking forward. I get so mad. (Portuguese-born, female office cleaner, age nineteen)

Just as working conditions can vary on the basis of sex rather than ability, they also vary on the basis of race. Although jobs are not apportioned on the basis of race, Black women at the post office in particular are most often targeted for differential treatment on the basis of sex and race and are regularly slurred by company officials, supervisors, and even occasionally co-workers:

> But the inspector John, he is a man, Greek. He always tell us mean things. He used to call us Black women whores in Greek until our Greek friend, Cia, tell us what it mean. We think is something friendly. We can't believe. (Guyanese-born, female "light duty" cleaner, age fifty-six)

Despite their goodwill and solidarity, even union officials at the post office are unaware of how their own internalized sexism, racism, and ethnocentrism favours the flow of information to some workers and not to others.

Divisions and Resistance

When asked to describe their jobs, office cleaners may not be able to articulate all the intricacies of the subcontracting process, the commodification of housework, or how gender, race, class, and sexuality are used to regulate their work. However, cleaners will readily tell anyone willing to listen that they experience a lack of respect, low wages, poor working conditions, a divided workforce, limited job security, and difficulties in organizing as cleaners:

> If I was the owner of this cleaning company I would make sure my supervisors knew as much about cleaning as my cleaners did. If I was a supervisor I would not just sit down, I would go and help cleaners. And I would pay cleaners more money. If the post office would take over from the contractor. . . we would have benefits and job security. (Yugoslavian-born, female "light duty" cleaner on rotating shifts, age forty-five)

> The cleaning companies are making a killing when it comes to paying the cleaners. (Colombian-born, male cleaner, age seventy-two)

They express a practical feeling for how subcontracting as an employment practice and their devaluation as women and immigrants is consequential to their daily devaluation as low-waged workers.

> People . . . need to see how cleaners feel. Because we feel like a piece of manure. Even though some of us do other things we still feel like nothing as cleaners. (Portuguese-born, female high school student and night cleaner, age eighteen)

Cleaners who previously worked in the direct employ of building owners rather than subcontractors have seen how their jobs changed over time because of the practice of subcontracting and privatization. Women have also seen how their waged cleaning work in the market is devalued in ways that are both similar and dissimilar to cleaning work in their own homes and how this devaluation enables private contractors to make profits at their expense. In defence of the value of her work, one woman said:

> People think cleaning is a low job. Cleaning is not a low job. Because if you don't clean how is the place going to get clean and tidy? (Guyanese-born, female cleaner, cleans early evening shift, age fifty-eight)

The rights of management to subcontract in a competitive labour market reinforces the already established social distance between different types of workers in places like the university and post office. Subcontracting not only socially insulates building management from cleaners and their demands for changes but also institutionally blurs the lines of communication and authority for subcontracted employees. The ambiguity of who is ultimately responsible for building-management decisions—building owners, building managers, or subcontracted cleaning firms—makes it difficult for cleaners to know where to channel their legitimate demands or complaints.

If cleaners at the university, for example, want to remedy sexual harassment they experience from security guards, students, or staff, they might need to complain not only to the cleaning company management and the security management but also to the university management. Yet despite the public and politicized nature of new sexual harassment policies, cleaners do not fall within the university guidelines for complaints on sexual harassment because they are neither in the direct employ nor students of the university. Even if the cleaning company management was willing to act on a complaint, it has no jurisdiction over security, students, or staff of the university and no institutional means to discipline harassers who are not other cleaners. The contract-cleaning company therefore has no authority to make changes in the workplace setting in which the cleaners work. The university may provide policies to protect people from harassment in the university setting but it does not consider contract workers such as cleaners to be a part of the university community in the way that students, staff, and faculty are.

Despite both workplace divisions and cultural/linguistic differences, post office cleaners were able to unionize at the post office under the leadership of a militant union. This was in contrast to the university cleaners who were unable to unionize even though other unionized, downtown office-building cleaners were organized with assistance from the Portuguese community.[13] The strategic importance of large numbers of cleaners, who were relatives and neighbours, employed in a small geographic proximity in the large buildings downtown facilitated the unionization of cleaners. Contrary to some popular opinions about women as unionists, even immigrant women, whether divided or not by cultural and class origins, whether socially distanced and isolated from each other as well as other workers, demonstrated that they will take part in militant strikes when required and when conditions make it possible.

Notes

1. The Hawley Group, for example, is a British multinational service corporation with offices in Toronto, known for its anti-union activities.

2. The Committee for Cleaner's Rights is a coalition of trade union and community groups and includes both women and men representing the Ontario Federation of Labour, the Canadian Union of Postal Workers, the Canadian Union of Public Employees, Food and Service Workers of Canada, the Labourers International Union, Local 183, the Ontario Public Service Employees International Union, the Southern Ontario Newspaper Guild, St. Christopher's Community House, the National Action Committee on the

Status of Women, and the Portuguese Inter-Agency Network.

3. From a meeting between Wendy Isler of the Food and Service Workers of Canada and an official of the Ontario Government, November 1986.

4. The average operating costs of downtown office buildings in Toronto, including energy costs, were estimated at $8.09 per square foot and cleaners' wages were only $0.74 of this figure (Committee for Cleaners' Rights, "Meeting" with the Hon. Gregory Sorbara, Minister of Labour, May 18, 1988," Part One Synopsis, p. 4, 1988).

5. Ghosting occurs when employers let positions go unfilled even though the contract states a certain number of positions are required to provide the cleaning service. On rare occasions contractors pay casual employees to fill the ghost positions, usually they simply intensify the work so that a lesser number of employees are actually working.

6. Joy Parr (1990), for example, has considered how the history of social and economic change accompanying industrialization in Ontario has affected women. Cohen (1988) has provided historical evidence on how women have shaped the economy and how patriarchal relations have also historically constrained women's participation in the economy in Ontario. Marjorie Cohen's work also demonstrates how in the Canada–United States Free Trade Agreement, women in the service sector have been disadvantaged by economic policies and economic restructuring (1987).

7. The similar ways that subcontracting is used in the cleaning industry in other industrialized countries is explored by Gowen (1988). For the British context see Coyle (1985).

8. O'Keefe Centre (1984), Connestoga College and Toronto Dominion Centre (1985), First Canadian Place (1986), Elizabeth Bruyere Centre (1986), Aetna Building (1986), Ontario Science Centre (1986), and the Scarborough Postal Plant (1986) cleaners had varying degrees of success in their strikes.

9. My thanks to Sheila MacIntyre, Faculty of Law, Queen's University, Kingston, Ontario for her work in pointing out how male dominance functions in legal theory and practice, specifically in labour law in Canada (personal correspondence, 1987). Catharine MacKinnon (1983), in particular, has been influential in theorizing how apparently neutral social systems have actually been formed and shaped by the dominant interests of men. For a discussion of how "skill" as a definition has been used to devalue women's work and knowledge, see Phillips and Taylor (1980). For a Canadian treatment of how concepts such as skill and competency are used in job-training programs, see Jackson (1986).

10. Anderson (1983) documents the labour market practices of the Canadian government that structured immigration to Canada in the 1950s and 1960s. The pattern of drawing rural Azoreans to Anglophone Canada and Toronto helped to supply a readily available labour market in the expanding cleaning industry. No other group has had the impact on the office cleaning industry that the Portuguese have had. For an examination of how migration, labour, and gender interact in the lives of Black women in Toronto see Dionne Brand (1984). For a review of the rationale behind the immigration of women to Canada see Alma Estable (1987) and for a graphic mapping of female

migration patterns see Joni Seager and Ann Olson (1986).

11. Cleaners ranged in age from their twenties to seventies at the post office, while university cleaners were much younger, ranging from the teens to late forties.

12. WHMIS is the abbreviation for the symbols designed and promoted through the Work Place Hazardous Materials Information System.

13. For a description and analysis of the 1984 Food and Service Workers of Canada (FASWOC) strike by primarily Portuguese-Canadian cleaners against Olympia and York's First Canadian Place, a downtown office complex containing both the Toronto Stock Exchange and the headquarters for the Bank of Montreal, see Hollingsworth (1986). The analytical framework underpinning the paper was based in part on work by Tilly (1981).

CHAPTER FIVE

"IT'S THE FOREIGNERS WHO DO THE LAUNDRY": THE WORK OF PORTUGUESE CHAMBERMAIDS IN LONDON HOTELS

Wenona Giles

Marlene is the soul of concern. She cannot sleep well at night unless she is certain you will. Her radiant smile belies a steely determination—to transform your room into a haven of tranquillity. With pillows the way you like them, French-milled soaps, and stacks of thick bath towels, morning and night. Like her untiring colleagues who press your jacket within the hour, polish your shoes overnight, and unfailingly take your phone messages, Marlene's mission is to enhance your personal comfort and, in turn, your professional efficiency the following day. Which makes a Four Seasons Hotel the kind of investment you never lose sleep over. (Four Seasons Hotel Advertisement 1991)

Introduction

In the above advertisement, the service provided by a hotel chamber maid takes on the character of a labour of love that recreates the "haven" of the home for a male clientele. The illusion is further developed by an accompanying photograph of a real person—a woman in a maid's uniform—whose identity is linked solely to the hotel: "Marlene Wei, Housekeeper, Four Seasons, Chicago." However, the selfless service offered by "Marlene Wei," is also sold as a good investment, a business deal between the client and the chambermaid. Reproductive labour, removed from the home into the market, must maintain its image of self-sacrifice and devotion while also appealing to the tenets of the market economy. The illusion is that the service being sold by the Four Seasons Corporation is qualitatively as good as, and perhaps better than, the services offered by unpaid and devoted mothers and wives. The other side of the illusory coin is that the only way that this work can be done for profit is by exploiting workers like "Marlene." The specific social relations and hierarchical structure of the work process in which hotel chambermaids engage provide the basis for the development of the illusion of the "haven of tranquillity" in a hotel room.

This chapter explores the links between the work of hotel chamber-maids and the employment of Portuguese women migrant workers in London, England. The marketing of hotel rooms is part of a multinational industry that has similar characteristics throughout the world. Like "Marlene," Portuguese women in London are employed for low wages and poor working conditions to provide the necessary services for hotel clients. It is important to move beyond the workplace to address how Portuguese women's identity is shaped through, not only their wage work, but also through their participation in non-wage work and gender relations outside the workplace. The culture that Portuguese women bring to the workplace and its contribution to challenging and changing the social relations of this industry are examined.

The hotel industry in London, England, relies in large part on the labour of migrant workers and women for accomplishing its lowest-paid work. At the time of fieldwork in 1982-84, Portuguese migrant women workers were only able to gain entry to Britain to work as paid domestic help, and thus most Portuguese in London are employed in the hotel and catering industry (Harris 1978; Giles 1987). The total population of Portuguese in the U.K. was approximately thirty thousand in 1981 (Runnymede Trust 1984:13). At that time, London, itself, had a total population of approximately ten thousand Portuguese (estimate by Centro 25 do Abril). The numbers of Portuguese in London have increased since the early 1980s, as many continue to enter for the first time and others return for a second time. These workers have formed a vulnerable and readily accessible group of labourers for hotel employers.

Chambermaids, as suppliers of laundry, and cooks, waiters, and waitresses provide the labour that shapes hotels into major sites of social reproduction.[1] Hotels are also in the business of creating profit from this process, and this is done by paying as little as possible to those workers who are on the lowest rungs of the hotel hierarchy. While the alleged (and advertised) role of the hotel is to service hotel clients, hotel owners cannot do this without producing a profit, resulting in a contraposition between their own self interest and the interests of their clients. This is resolved by relying on workers who will carry out this labour for low wages and under poor working conditions. One of the ironies of this relationship is that the reproductive needs of the workers themselves receive little attention from the hotel owners. When carried out at home, reproductive labour is located outside the market and has no cost attached to it. When it is done outside the home, for example, in a fast-food restaurant or hotel, or by cleaners in a public building, it takes on a value that depends only partly on the price paid for this labour. The more important calculation is the level of exploitation that the employer can maintain *vis-à-vis* the worker and still ensure that these workers return to their jobs each day.

The hotel hierarchy is underpinned by the association of hotel work with a racial/ethnic and gendered categorization of the workforce. In the eyes of hotel owners, clients, and ultimately the wider society, Portuguese women, among other ethnic minorities, are imbued with identities that are associated with the lowest-paid jobs in hotels. They are regarded in a unidimensional way as wage workers, whose own reproductive needs are minimized in the eyes of their employers.

The gendered nature of work in general locates women in some jobs and not others and places them at the bottom of hierarchical work organizations (Hartmann 1976; Beechey 1987; Acker 1988; Fudge and McDermott 1991). Acker argues that because the gender order is so embedded in the hierarchical work structure, any suggestion of change is perceived as a threat to the hierarchy itself (482). Race and ethnic identity supplies another layer of distinction (Meintel et al. 1985; Boyd 1990; Bottomley, de Lepervanche, and Martin 1991; Yuval-Davis 1991). Thus women of some ethnic groups are more rigidly defined into the lower ends of workplace hierarchical structures.

Explorations of how national, ethnic, and racial categories are created are central to understanding why specific groups are associated with particular kinds of wage work. Yuval-Davis and Anthias (1989) critique narrow definitions of reproduction that focus on biological reproduction, the reproduction of labour power, or state citizenship. Instead they call for analyses of the reproduction of national, ethnic, and racial categories. The association of the work of hotel chambermaid, with a group such as Portuguese migrant women attests to the need for a broader understanding of how these categories get reproduced.

Hotel and catering trades have clung to rigid hierarchies and to traditional work processes and technologies as other industries have become more innovative. This suggests that when done for pay and under capitalist conditions, housekeeping work defies post-Fordist forms of worker organization. In other words, when this work is done for profit, it demands a low-paid, tightly controlled workforce, whereas the more modern technical systems incorporate "flatter" hierarchies, greater "lateral" communication, and accelerated technological innovation (Rustin

1989:56-58).[2] This would explain why hotel owners require a vulnerable workforce—women, immigrants, migrants, youth, and illegal workers—a group whose needs and creative power can be more easily subordinated to the drive for profit (Elson 1988; Luxton and Maroney 1992). The work of reproduction that is managed by hotel owners occurs on the backs of the chambermaids, waiters, and other service workers. This work is identified with certain ethnic/racial groups and particularly with women, and this identification is associated with a devaluation of their labour power.

The Hotel Industry and Migrant Workers in London

Foreign workers have been sought by the hotel industry since the 1950s; however, it was after 1970 in the U.K. that the major growth in hotel jobs began. In the 1960s the number of overseas visitors to the U.K. more than doubled, due to the increase in tourism and the devaluation of the British pound (Dronfield and Soto 1981). Tourism became a significant source of employment, and the British government responded by initiating the Hotel Development Incentive Scheme, providing a grant of up to £1,000 per room in every new hotel built (1981:10). There were more hotels constructed in the five years between 1969 and 1974 than from the turn of the century to 1970[3] (Medlik 1978). It was in this phase that large and luxurious group-owned hotels were established, particularly in London, many of them having bought out smaller hotels during the recession in the mid-1970s (Dronfield and Soto 1981). In the 1980s ten companies owned approximately one-third of all the hotel bedspaces in London.

However, in 1977, 56 percent of hotel workers were still employed in small hotels, mainly in the provinces outside of London (Medlik 1978), where workers were isolated and confronted the least technologically-advanced working conditions. Dronfield and Soto (1981) argue that large corporations exploited the low wages and poor working conditions set by the small hotels to keep their own wages down and to increase their profits.

The increase in the number of hotels meant an increased demand for labour from the late 1960s onwards, especially in the large luxury hotels in London. In 1971, as the major growth in hotel jobs in the U.K. began, just under 50 percent of hotel workers in London were migrants: "Hotels and restaurants employed a higher proportion of foreigners than any other industry" (Medlik 1978:16).[4] While the number of work permits was declining by the early 1970s due to the tightening of immigration controls, it is significant to note that hotel workers were among the groups of workers excluded from a ban on the entry of unskilled and semi-skilled labour. In other words, this group of workers was singled out for special status. However, from 1972 onward, the quota was progressively reduced under pressure from the Trade Union Congress that insisted that the service industry should hire from among the country's unemployed. But, because of the difficulty of recruiting local labour to work in this industry, employers protested strongly against the reduction of the quota. In 1977, the government made the racist announcement that non-European women were no longer to be permitted entry to work as resident domestics (Bhabha, Klug, and Shutter 1985:132-133). In addition, Department of Employment policies reiterated that in a time of high unemployment, employers should hire local labour.

By 1979, the quota for unskilled and semi-skilled permits for the service industry was officially ended and in 1980, the quota for resident domestics was abolished. This meant that hotel employers could no longer rely on legal immigration for workers, and so turned to illegal migrant workers, who are more vulnerable to poor working conditions and pay. Confronting a shortage of hotel workers, employers did try to seek labour elsewhere than in the migrant population. Hotel companies sent what were called "mobile job shops" to areas of high unemployment in London and recruitment campaigns were also launched in cities characterized by high unemployment such as Liverpool and Glasgow. However, the levels of wages, conditions of work, hours, and social status of work in the service industry did not attract many unemployed British workers.[5]

In the U.K., legal migrant workers are essentially "tied" for four years to the type of work for which their initial permit was arranged.[6] They may change employers, but not job description. Changing jobs requires that the new employer write to the Department of Employment for a permit. The work permit is issued to the employer, not the migrant, for a specific job and a certain period, usually no more than a year.

> When I first came here there were agencies that would find jobs for migrants if you paid them £200. The problem was that most Portuguese would come here on visitor's permits and it is really only the employer who can get you a work permit. (Amelia,[7] age thirty-five)

Unemployed migrants are liable for deportation. Thus, because of their reliance on employers, migrants are highly vulnerable to workplace exploitation. In addition, during the first four years of their residence in the U.K., workers risk deportation if they engage in any form of political protest. These migrant workers, therefore, are a kind of captive or indentured labour force:[8]

When you have a work permit, you cannot go on strike [for four years]. So when I joined the picket line with the other chambermaids at the Grosvenor Hotel a few years ago, the police came to find me. I had to "disappear" from that picket line and search for work down the road at the Britannia Hotel. (Amelia, age thirty-five)

The effect of the ban on the immigration of unskilled and semi-skilled workers in the U.K. has been an increase in the number of illegal workers. In some cases employers and employment agencies recruit workers who have officially come to the U.K. as visitors. Workers pay a fee to employment agencies that arrange illegal jobs for them in the U.K. The agency then applies for a work permit for the migrant. This application is likely to be turned down because the immigration rules disallow those who enter the country as visitors from staying on as workers. In many cases, workers have been traced and arrested as a result of this application. The ambiguity in the British immigration law, i.e., on the one hand, discouraging unskilled workers, but on the other hand, allowing employers to apply for work permits for migrant workers, leaves workers in highly vulnerable situations.

The Social Relations of Hotel Work

Patterns of employment in hotels are arranged for maximum flexibility, through employment practices that leave individual workers with few legal rights and limited opportunities for collective organization (Byrne 1986:53). Flexibility is underpinned by the fact that over 60 percent of the hotel and catering workforce are women (this compares with 44 percent of the British economy as a whole employing women) (1986:15). Ten percent of the hotel and catering workforce are foreign nationals—the majority of whom come from countries such as the Philippines, Turkey, and Portugal (15). Few of this 10 percent are located in managerial or skilled areas of work.

The hotel and catering industry is the worst-paying industry in the U.K. (Dronfield and Soto 1981:4). For a single person in the U.K. with no children or other dependants, "the poverty line" by 1985 was equivalent to earnings of £88 per week.[9] In April 1985, three fifths of all women manual hotel and catering workers and one third of male manual hotel and catering workers had fallen below this level (Byrne 1986:6). The earnings used in this calculation included overtime.

These figures exclude part-time workers and young workers (under twenty-one years). Women form the majority of part-time workers in the hotel and catering industry and just under half of all workers in this industry are women part-time workers (1986:15). Part-time workers, that is, ones who work less than sixteen hours a week, lack the bargaining power of fulltime staff and earn on average proportionately less than their fulltime counterparts. They often lose entitlement to sick pay and maternity and unemployment benefits (1986:16).

Young people are increasingly being hired into this industry because they can be paid lower rates than adult workers. In 1983, 15 percent of the hotel and catering workforce was aged between sixteen and twenty-one years (Byrne 1986:19). However, job turnover is very high, with a yearly general turnover in hotels and guest houses of 70 percent of all workers of all ages (1986:2). Young workers are a significant part of this turnover: as they reach twenty-one years of age and must be paid a higher minimum wage, they are made redundant. Byrne describes hotel work as characterized by high levels of casualisation, part-time work, labour turnover, and employer hostility (1986:53n).

The Devaluation of a Chambermaid's Work

In the same way that women's work is devalued in relation to men's work in other sectors (Acker 1988), women's wages in hotels are consistently less than men's wages for doing what needs to be considered work of equal value. Wages are determined by "skill" levels. The work of cleaning that women do in hotels is often described as being less skilled than, for example, waiting on tables. Gaskell describes the process of evaluating skills as "highly political, contextual, and ideological" and states that there is a relationship between power relations and skill designations, such that skill categories are "used to justify and challenge existing hierarchies at work" (1991:143). In 1985, the job description of a head housekeeper in a 210-bedroom hotel in London, receiving £110 per week for working forty-five hours, includes the following tasks:

> ...ensures that the hotel has a constant supply of clean, lettable rooms; supervises the laundry and much of the hotel's cleaning operation; controls stocks of linen, cleaning materials, and equipment, baby cots, Bibles; and undertakes personnel management for 27 staff—including staff interviews, completing time sheets, calculating weekly bonus payments. (Pearson 1985:118)

In his research on U.K. hotels, Pearson found that the job of the restaurant manager in a hotel is considered by many hotel owners to be at the same level as the head housekeeper, however this person (usually a male) is paid £135 per week. In fact he is only responsible for nine staff and his main duties are supervision of the waiters and checking the till. As Pearson points out the only possible reason for the difference in pay scale is that the head housekeeper is classified as a female job and the restaurant manager as a male job. Job classification is used to affirm low pay and discriminates against women. A 1981 study (Dronfield and Soto), found that 56 percent of fulltime hotel staff and 90 percent of part-time staff had jobs that were considered unskilled or semi-skilled compared with only 20 percent of the general workforce (1981:3). The jobs done by women in hotels were nearly always considered unskilled (see Bhabha et al. 1985; Harris 1978; Maldonada 1983). Approximately 90 percent of the women I interviewed were in jobs that were classified as unskilled.

Female migrant workers are located at the bottom of this descending hierarchy and while some migrant men may have "semi-skilled" or "skilled" jobs, migrant women are consistently located in "unskilled" work, for which they receive low wages. Hotels and restaurants have developed job hierarchies that serve to maintain segregation by sex and migrant minority group membership. These divisions challenge the potential for worker unity in a situation in which all workers, regardless of rank, are highly exploited.

Working Conditions of Portuguese Chambermaids

Relationships between hotel chambermaids and clients are generally more impersonal than those in some other forms of domestic work, such as that of childcare workers or domestics in private homes (see Rollins 1985; Glenn 1986; Palmer 1989). Chambermaids are not in an employer—employee relationship with hotel clients and in fact have limited personal contact with these clients. Rather they are part of a hierarchical workforce in the employ of hotel managers\owners. Their cleaning work is evaluated by hotel managers and their wage is determined by these managers\owners. Their situation is similar to the work of subcontracting described by Neal in chapter four—the tiered working conditions regulated by "masculinist legislation" and "creating divisions based on gender, race, ethnicity, class, and sexuality."

Portuguese migrant women who work as chambermaids in hotels describe their work as exhausting and, in general, they express dislike for the work. But they have also found ways of challenging the hierarchical social relations of their workplace, including strikes, leaving their jobs, and working collectively rather than in isolation. They are cognizant of the fact that it is a segregated workforce, where migrant women occupy the lowest rungs of the hierarchy:

In the U.K. it is the foreigners who do the laundry. (Ilda, age forty-five)

Without English and from a non-EEC country, the only jobs available [for us] are service jobs. When you have a work permit, you have to do hard labour for five years and then you can do as you like. (Amelia, age thirty-five)

In a large hotel, a chambermaid may clean from ten to fifteen rooms a day plus extra rooms when a co-worker is ill or has a day off. She generally works alone, unless a friend is working on the same floor, in which case the two will try to work together on empty rooms while waiting for other rooms to be vacated. Not only is this often a more efficient method of cleaning, but it also challenges the isolating organization of the work. Like unpaid domestic work in the home, cleaning in hotels is carried out with inefficient and outdated labour-intensive equipment or no equipment at all. Pearson (1985:33) describes the hotel working conditions in the words of a head housekeeper at the Grand Hotel in London:

> We've old hoovers and we've no trolleys for the maids. There is no service lift or linen chute so they have to hump the linen on their backs from the sixth floor down. They're like wee pack horses going about. They're [the hotel owners] wanting efficiency to help improve the service, but they won't help us do so.

Employers frequently take advantage of chambermaids by asking them to work longer hours and do extra chores, the expectation being, that if they do not do the work, they will be let go. Some chambermaids challenge these expectations by turning the tables on employers in this regard. As one chambermaid said, she never worked in the same hotel for more than three years,

> because then they start to ask you to do all sorts of things that you don't want to do and that are extra to your normal load. (Paula, age thirty-nine)

The hierarchy to which a chambermaid answers in a luxury hotel runs from her immediate superior—a "floor supervisor"—to an "assistant head housekeeper," an "executive head housekeeper," and a "general manager." Each of these persons is somehow involved in overseeing the work of the chambermaid. The quality of the cleaning job is emphasized more or less depending upon the importance of the client:

> When there is a VIP guest, the room gets special attention and is cleaned especially well. It is then checked by the floor supervisor,

the assistant head housekeeper, the executive head housekeeper, and the guest relations manager. And each one screams at the other. (Maria, age thirty-two)

A 1981 study describes the pay scale in a large London hotel as following the hierarchy Maria describes. A chambermaid earned from £40 to £75 a week (less than $10,000 a year), a floor supervisor earned £85, an assistant head housekeeper earned £95, a head housekeeper earned £100, and a guest relations manager earned £230. The industry's directors paid themselves over £1000 a week and a hotel's profits may run to millions of pounds a year (Dronfield and Soto 1981). In 1985 the legal minimum rate for adult workers in the hotel and catering industry was around £70 a week. However the Wages Inspectorate found that in 37.3 percent of the licensed hotels and restaurants visited in that year, the employer was paying workers less than the legal minimum rate (Byrne 1986:5).

Low wages are related to the competitive nature of this industry, where in some cases departments are encouraged to vie with one another for staying below their budgets:

> Each department has their own budget and the contest is to see how well they can stay within that budget. Every three months they have to answer on paper what they've spent. (Amelia, age thirty-five)

The small-town, family-run hotels can also be oppressive places to work. Isolation from a community of fellow workers can contribute to the difficulties that workers confront. In one such situation, a young Portuguese woman, Anna, arrived in Britain with a work permit for a job in a small hotel in the Yorkshire countryside:

> I earned £4.70 a week [approximately $8 a week in 1972] and worked from 8 a.m. to 6 p.m. in the hotel as a chambermaid. I think I was a slave. After three months, the owner asked me to work in the hotel bakery from 8 p.m. to 5 a.m. as well as cleaning during the day in the hotel. Well I don't know when he thought I was going to sleep. I just couldn't manage this and quit after a week. I didn't know where I was and couldn't speak any English. I found my way back to London somehow and moved in with friends for awhile. But my boss went to the Portuguese consulate—he thought he could force me back to work because he had signed my work permit papers for me. (Anna, age twenty-five)

In fact, the employer could not legally force Anna back to work for him and she found employment elsewhere. However, I was told of similar cases where immigration officials maliciously informed migrants that they would be deported if they left the jobs they had been given on entry into the country.

Employers often justify low wages by arguing that their staff receive a subsidy in the form of rent and food. However, many Portuguese complained of the inadequacy of their living conditions:

> We left our children in Portugal and had jobs in Dorset cleaning a hotel. But there was hardly any food for us. I started to get headaches and we both started to lose too much weight. We soon had to leave that job and go to London to stay with friends there. (Suzanna, age thirty-eight)

It is mainly those women who come without husband or children to the U.K. who live at their place of work. A study done in 1978 (Ramsay) states that one in five workers in the hotel industry live in. These live-in workers are mainly women working as domestics: 52 percent of housekeepers, 43 percent of chambermaids, 40 percent of receptionists, and 31 percent of bar staff. The accommodation is substandard and a third of the women share a room. Complaints range from frequent breakdowns in heating and hot water, unsanitary conditions and no lighting in bathrooms, and insufficient and poor quality food to surveillance of workers' guests: "Altogether, it's like living in a mental home" (Dronfield and Soto 1981:5). Workers are charged anywhere from a third to a half of their wages for room and board. Employers are allowed to deduct £4.80 a week from workers wages for food that is often substandard. One worker at the Grand Hotel described the staff food as:

> ... diabolical. It's sausages, beans and chips today, a one-course, one-choice meal, or eat a sandwich. We have not had soup for ages. They even put a note by the milk machine saying staff are not allowed to drink the milk. (Pearson 1985:34)

Those who "live in" are frequently asked to increase their workload for no extra income and run the risk of dismissal or eviction if they refuse. A survey by Knight (1978) discovered that 55 percent of the workers living in were working over fifty hours a week compared with only 10 percent for the industry as a whole. Portuguese female hotel cleaning staff expressed a dislike of live-in arrangements and aspired to a council flat, apartment, or room of their own as soon as it was affordable and available.

Immigration officials often make it more difficult for those who are living at their place of work to change employment:

> Living in creates restrictions regarding changing jobs and the Home Office is more reluctant to give permission to change jobs to those who live in. (Julio, age forty-nine)

Strikes and Struggles

Labour disputes have been common in the hotel industry in London, particularly in the large multinational hotel chains, such as the Trusthouse Forte Group and Metropolitan hotels. Portuguese workers have frequently taken part in strikes at the hotels, in spite of the risks involved for migrant labour. This political activity has brought Portuguese together from time to time to act collectively in their own interests and in the wider interests of other migrant and non-migrant workers. But taking political action has not been an easy decision for many Portuguese workers. One young Portuguese chambermaid described the different attitudes among older and younger workers:

> Really, we are all here producing for the U.K. as cheap labour. We are told that if we aren't prepared to do it, we should go home. The older generation accepts the situation as natural, but the younger generation is more rebellious. But in fact we all have little choice. Where I work now at the Europa, the workers are all afraid that if they lose their jobs, they won't be able to find other ones. (Amelia, age thirty-five)

One of the most significant political movements instigated by the Portuguese in London occurred in the early 1970s, when about fifty Portuguese hotel and catering workers, who were part of a group called the "LIGA" (The Portuguese Educational and Cultural League), formed a committee of the Transport and General Workers Union called the *Portuguese Workers' Branch*. The Portuguese were quickly joined by Turkish, Spanish, Greek, and other foreign workers and consequently changed their name to the International Workers' Branch. The formation of this Branch contributed to the increase in strike activity in hotels and restaurants in the 1970s. Within months of the establishment of the Branch in 1972, fifteen hundred members were recruited among Portuguese, Spanish, Greek, Turkish, and Arabic workers. One Portuguese man reminisced:

> There were strikes everywhere from '71 to '74! In the beginning

the unions couldn't get into the hotels because of the language problem. But when the International Worker's Branch was organized by the Portuguese, all the union and strike information came to us in our own languages. People walked out at Wimpey's, the Carleton Towers Hotel, the Angus Steak Houses. The Talk of the Town had to close. (Saul, age forty-six)

In a strike at Grosvenor House, a Trusthouse Forte hotel, in 1979, thirty women lost their jobs as chambermaids. Fifteen of them, some who had lived there for more than fifteen years, were evicted from their accommodation in the hotel with forty-eight hours notice. In 1983, waiters in the same hotel were on strike again.

The years spanning the late 1970s and early 1980s were also a time of important political change in Portugal, just prior to and following the 1974 revolution there. In 1973, when Prime Minister Caetano came to London, the Portuguese organized demonstrations against his visit throughout London, using the International Workers' Branch as a networking device. The specific historical circumstances in Portugal played some part in radicalizing the Portuguese at this time in London.[10]

The history of Portugese women's struggles as chambermaids is related to their own political history involving the socialist revolution in their country. Most of the Portuguese in London are from mainland Portugal, where the revolution had its greatest impact. They have maintained close ties with Portugal through kin relationships, through annual returns, and through migration projects to retire in Portugal. As well, their personal history as members of the working class in Portugal before they migrated is important. The majority of Portuguese migrant women in London worked in wage jobs before migrating. Twenty-one per cent of those interviewed were engaged in paid domestic work in Portugal and others were employed in a variety of jobs, including teaching/tutoring, factory work, piece work at home, hairdressing, secretarial work, and agricultural labour. A number of women had migrated alone and until recently a greater number of Portuguese migrants to London have been women. I have argued that Portuguese women's pre-migration experience as members of the working class has also had a significant effect on their level of worker consciousness and gender consciousness (Giles 1992).

Conclusion

To the extent that Portuguese women can resist the imposition of inequality, they have done so, even risking their jobs and accommodation, by engaging in strikes. Participation in hotel work has left these women and their families economically vulnerable, reinforcing gender inequalities inside and outside of the household. Thus, defining women's status requires an understanding of those social relations that extend beyond the workplace. Similarly, women's efforts at resistance extend beyond the workplace and into their neighbourhoods and households. Elsewhere, I have discussed how Portuguese women initiated a struggle for better housing in their neighbourhood (Giles 1991). I argue that this struggle was related to the sense of opposition that women had developed in their wage work. Likewise, I have also discussed how women express opposition to their status as migrant workers through less visible forms of resistance, such as return orientation[11] and gender struggles in the household (Giles 1992). The majority of Portuguese married women interviewed in London regarded returning to Portugal as a desirable alternative to what they described as unsatisfactory work and domestic situations in London. Women went so far as to speak about leaving their husbands in order to return to Portugal.

It is important to examine a variety of forms of resistance, many that are not necessarily overt or visible.[12] Women's identities as Portuguese, migrant, and wage worker are defined by their associations with their households and by their engagement in a particular form of hotel work. Based on her own research of migrant women from the former Yugoslavia, Morokvasic states that migrant women "resist rather than take their situation for granted" and this resistance lays the basis for change (1991:81). However, she argues that migration and access to paid employment does not necessarily lead to an improvement in women's status or more egalitarian gender relations (1991:82). Likewise, Yuval-Davis states that participation in the public domain is not necessarily accompanied by a higher degree of empowerment. In order to understand the social relations of paid domestic work as well as the struggles of Portuguese women who do this work in hotels in London, we need to examine how gender divisions of labour and ethnic patterns of cultural hegemony are formed in society (1991:66). Through their expressions of discontent and their sometimes covert forms of resistance, Portuguese chambermaids demonstrate both an awareness of workplace and household inequalities, as well as a certain sense of empowerment through their struggles.

It is the relationship between reproduction in all its forms and production that must be further explored in order to understand how women develop a self-conscious resistance to gender, class, and ethnic/racial inequalities. Labour struggles arise most often through conflicts over distribution (jobs and higher wages), rather than over the control of production (Acker 1988), and Portuguese chambermaids participate actively in this struggle for jobs and higher wages. But we need to understand how these jobs and wages are imbued with gender as well as ethnic/racial inequalities. Portuguese women's resistance in the workplace is related to cross-cutting identities and other forms of resistance in their households and communities, as well as their personal and collective histories.

Portuguese women are cognizant of the power of employers and the British state, and they recognize their work as undervalued. They are aware of the irony of taking care of others and not having their own needs for adequate food and shelter addressed. Out of this awareness and their struggles in other domains—in their households, neighbourhoods, and their relationship with the politics of Portugal—has arisen a critical perspective of their status as women, migrants, and working class. It is from this kind of perspective that the ground is laid for larger, more encompassing struggles.

Acknowledgement

Research for chapter five, by Wenona Giles, was carried out in London and Portugal under the auspices of a Social Science Research Council of Canada Fellowship and a York University Research Grant.

Notes

1. The term "social reproduction" or "reproductive labour" refers in a general way to the four main work processes that ensure the survival of individuals and households: the reproduction of the labour power of the wage earner and the domestic worker, childbearing and rearing, housework and the transformation of wages into goods and services (Luxton 1980:18). In their paid jobs, hotel workers engage in the reproduction of the labour of the wage earner and the housework entailed in this endeavour.
2. However, as Reiter points out in her chapter on the fast food industry, the "team concept" has been used to thwart union organizing and the worker collectivity is often defined by management.
3. The construction of hotels—as opposed to individually run "inns" began at the turn of the century.
4. See also Campbell-Platt 1976; Harris 1978; Freeman and Spencer 1979; Maldonada 1983; The U.K. Dept. of Employment Gazette 1925–1980.
5. Sassen-Koob's (1985) research in N.Y. supports these findings. She states that non-immigrant workers in New York are socialized to expect better working conditions and thus refuse to take low-status and low-wage jobs that immigrants *will* take. Those non-immigrant workers who do take these jobs tend to be regarded as "unreliable" or as dissatisfied workers—thus they are not as attractive to employers as migrants.
6. Until Portugal's official entry to the E.E.C. in 1992, Portuguese were part of this group of migrants. It is not yet clear how this changed status will affect Portuguese workers.
7. All names used in this chapter are pseudonyms.

8. The status of these workers is similar to domestic workers in Canada who enter under the Domestic Workers Scheme, whereby they are tied to a specific type of job—domestic work (mainly as nannies)—for two years before they can apply for landed-immigrant status. On the one hand, immigration officials defend this program as privileging a group of women who would not otherwise be able to gain entry to Canada under the points system. On the other hand, they state privately that if the points system were altered to give points for paid domestic work, "domestic workers would not stay in those jobs once they received resident status and there would be a dearth of private domestics" (conversation with policy analyst of the Department of Immigration in 1992.

9. This figure is 140 percent of the Supplementary Benefit for a person living alone, and has been calculated as the minimum income necessary to avoid social deprivation (see Byrne 1986; Mack and Lansley 1985).

10. Likewise, Bookman (1988) discusses the development of a union movement in an electronics factory in Boston, and states that for the first generation Portuguese workers who made up one third of the workforce in that factory, the revolution in Portugal, with which they identified, provided an important political backdrop to their resistance.

11. In my research among Portuguese women in London, I found that women more than men expressed a strong desire to return to Portugal and I have argued that this is an expression of resistance to the gender relations and working conditions they experienced in London as opposed to Portugal (Giles 1992).

12. See also Lamphere 1987.

CHAPTER SIX

THE FAST FOOD INDUSTRY: PUTTING THE FAMILY TO WORK

Ester Reiter

Introduction

Producing and cooking food for the family/household has long been the responsibility of women, assisted by their children. Early critics identified one of the causes of women's oppression as their subordination to the cooking stove, and both Marxist and feminist visionaries sought to achieve women's equality through removing such work from the private sphere of the family (Lenin 1972; Hayden 1981). The socialist and feminist solutions, however, for various reasons never became widespread. Ironically, it was within the sphere of capital expansion that the family dinner was removed from the home. Until quite recently, approximately twenty-five years ago, people ate their meals away from home only when absolutely necessary. Restaurants were not a substitute for the family gathered around the dinner table. Extensive advertising that was directed at the family created the notion that eating away from home was an acceptable and affordable alternative to the family dinner, and successfully changed eating habits (Reiter 1991).

Capital may have succeeded in getting the meal out of the kitchen, but the family members who have always had responsibility for its preparation have remained the same: women and teenagers form the workforce for part-time work in fast-food outlets. McDonald's, the largest of the hamburger chains, has pioneered an organization of work that successfully uses inexperienced women and teenagers in jobs for which they can be trained in a few hours. The unskilled, fast-paced nature of the work is regarded as a model for efficient and profitable industries, that is, an example of how to intensify work using minimum-wage labour. Indeed, "McJobs" has entered the North American lexicon, indicating that the kind of work women and young people do in fast-food restaurants may well be the typical job of the future.

This article draws upon my experience working in a Burger King outlet in a suburb of Toronto, Ontario, examines the nature of this work, and looks at some of the implications of the transfer of an activity from the unpaid sphere of production for use into a profitable undertaking. I explore the contradiction between an organization of work that provides a particularly intensive and stressful experience for the people who produce food and the marketing of a product that is based on telling women that they deserve to "give themselves a break today."

Fast-food is a very competitive industry and there are tremendous pressures on companies to grow and expand if they are to survive. If they are unable to increase their market share, then they fall by the wayside. The fast-food industry, in both marketing and management techniques, invokes family values of a particular North American variety. A great deal of money and effort is spent convincing the public that their fast-food restaurants are clean, healthful places to have a meal, and that these companies care about the community and their customers. Crew workers are expected to promote these views to help their employer increase sales.

When a diamond ring is advertised as a symbol of lasting commitment to marital bliss, the consumer is not shown pictures of men torn from their families to live in the mining compounds of South Africa. It would not be good for business. It is often left to consumers to figure out that it is not the "Jolly Green Giant," but Mexican workers, who live and work under appalling conditions, who produce "Green Giant" peas or broccoli. So too, the sale of fast-food as a fun, healthful dose of Americana makes invisible the actual conditions of work for the women and young people who work there. The environmental and nutritional aspects of this industry are ignored.

The introduction of the market into family dining (getting the family to eat in a fast-food restaurant) has been achieved by selling the notion of family for profit. Happiness and a wholesome way of life are part of the promise, and good parents will take their children out for a McDonald's or Burger King birthday party package. As employers, fast-food companies depend on and contribute to a patriarchal system that involves a very unequal distribution of wages for paid employment and lopsided responsibilities in nonwaged areas of reproductive labour. Companies paying these low wages ensure that women and teenagers will continue to consider themselves "not really" workers. Survival of the household is not possible without the wages of the "head" of the family, the main breadwinner.

International Growth

Since the major growth of the industry in the 1960s and 1970s, the North American market has become saturated with fast-food outlets, and domestically, these companies continue to seek out potential locations in hitherto untapped areas, such as hospitals, prisons, and schools, to enlarge their share of the market. An even more promising growth area is selling fast-food internationally. Large companies such as McDonald's, Grand Met PFC (which owns Burger King), and Pepsico (which owns Kentucky Fried Chicken and Pizza Hut) are increasingly looking to foreign markets. McDonald's estimates that 40 percent of their new units will be in overseas markets (*Nation's Restaurant News* 1988). Just as North Americans go to a fast-food chain because of the marketing, rather than the food, so also success in the international arena depends on the attractiveness of the image. People flock to fast-food restaurants to experience the American culture of consumerism. The fast-food industry has become a symbol of the wonders of what a free market can bring.

The 1990s are a time when all countries are encouraged to embrace the new religion, of the "free" or unregulated marketplace where the gospel is one of competitiveness. The mecca of this new religion lies in the United States, where the architects and policemen of the New World Order reside. The message is a global one, imparted with missionary zeal and assisted by some financial and military arm twisting.[1] The path to a better life is presented as a non-union paved road, designed in the U.S.A. Indeed throughout the world, American-style mass consumerism dominates the airwaves, the movie screens, and many people's fantasies.[2]

Fast food is an industry that is central to this new form of domination. American fast-food outlets such as Pepsico, McDonald's and Grand Met PFC are located throughout the world. While few of the citizens of second and third world countries can afford to buy such a meal, a hamburger, fries, and a Coke are considered a special treat. In Shanghai, a Kentucky Fried Chicken meal for one person (three pieces of chicken, fries, and a Pepsi) cost about fifteen yuan or almost one fifth of the monthly salary of an academic. In Mexico, the pesos required for a Big Mac, fries, and a Coke amount to approximately two full days' wages in a maquiladora. The thousands of people lined up for the opening of McDonald's in Moscow were hoping to have a taste of U.S. affluence through their Big Mac. Prices in Moscow, as in other places, far exceed what a worker could regularly afford to pay for a meal.

Thus, countries from Europe to the People's Republic of China to Mexico are all promising growth areas for the expansion of fast-food. Unlike other sectors (e.g., auto, steel, textiles, and food production), where North American jobs are threatened by the globalization of the firm there is no direct relationship between the disappearance of fast-food outlets in North America and their proliferation elsewhere in the world. The organization of work in this industry however has become a model adapted from industrial assembly-line work, to be used in other service industries, from education to health. The profitability of these companies is admired, and it is touted that the wealth of large transnationals will trickle down into the countries in which they are locating. Thus, a private, for-profit company that provides services using low-paid workers is considered a good, efficient way to run a business. The exploitative nature of these companies that allows them to be so profitable masquerades as technical know-how.

The reality, however, is quite different. In Mexico, for example, restrictions requiring foreign franchisers to use Mexican materials were lifted in 1990 and the foreign-based, fast-food industry is growing rapidly. Plans for privatizing Mexico's resources and many of its industries are well under way. In the midst of *Business Week*'s statement that the creation of a "boom market for U.S. goods in Latin America is a miracle cure" (*Business Week* Feb 10, 1992), the living standards of Mexican workers and peasants has fallen 60 percent since 1982 as a result of free trade and privatization. Twenty-five percent of Mexican women workers earn *less* than the minimum wage (Sinclair 1992).

Development of the Fast-Food Industry in Canada

Perhaps the implications of the worldwide growth of fast food can be better understood by looking at the first country that the U.S.-based companies targeted for expansion: Canada. The restaurant business in Canada was traditionally the kind of enterprise where a disproportionate number of proprietors were immigrants with little capital. Chinese, Macedonian, or Jewish immigrants, groups who confronted discriminatory treatment in getting factory jobs, often opened up their own businesses. Employees were either immigrants like themselves or young Canadian-born women coming to the city from rural backgrounds.[3] As the fast-food industry developed in the 1960s, the new restaurants became franchisees of large corporate structures for which the small family-run restaurants were no match. While they could certainly compete in food quality, the tremendous marketing advantage of the large corporations made staying in business very difficult. One company, McDonald's, controlled as much as 50 percent of the hamburger market in Canada by the mid-1980s (*Financial Post* August 25, 1984).

With this concentration in the industry, standardization of operations became necessary, and computer technology, applied both within outlets and centrally to devise a new type of labour process, made it possible.

Although restaurant work has always been labour intensive, McDonald's pioneered a way to make the worker into a "machine tender" and restaurant labour similar to jobs on an assembly line. Such an organization of the labour process allowed the most inexperienced and cheapest form of labour to be utilized. Part-time work was especially suitable for this industry where rush hours were only during meal times. In North America, such a labour force could be found within the family. Women who could not afford decent daycare or who found it difficult to manage fulltime paid work in addition to their home responsibilities found this kind of part-time work, close to home, attractive. Their teenage children were hired for the evenings and weekends. In the 1980s, when the companies had difficulty finding enough workers, they also sought to attract retirees (the grandparents) as workers (*Financial Post* August 25, 1984).

The close connection between paid work, unpaid work, and the world of consumption is illustrated in this industry. Large companies such as McDonald's and Burger King not only draw upon family members for their labour force, but through extensive advertising they also create a market for their products in the family. However, the for-profit sector is a less than ideal solution to the isolation and time-consuming nature of the work that women do at home. Eating out is part of a trend where more and more goods and services required by the family household need to be bought. To pay for them, women feel pressured to take on waged work. Because these goods and services are designed with profit, rather than the needs of the consumer, in mind, the quality of what is offered on the market is often less than satisfactory.

The Creation of the Consumer

The creation of a market for a "dining out experience" is part of the general transformation of social life which began in the post-World War One period in North America and accelerated during the post-World War Two era. By the 1950s, market specialists were learning that if there is no existing need for a product, then the challenge is to find one or create one. Restaurant sales increased during World War Two because people had jobs and money, many families were separated, and more women than ever were working. Amidst rather pessimistic speculation about what would happen to the industry once the war ended, one excited visionary wrote in the *Canadian Hotel and Restaurant Journal* about his discovery of the market in the home. While up until this time restaurant patronage was limited to those out for a special treat or people who could not be at home for dinner, the idea that one could promote eating out as a replacement for dinner at home, part of a family's normal eating habits, was a brilliant new insight:

It's [targeting the family at home] a magic that enables any restaurant to be as big as a city, to gather profits as big as the operator's imagination and to do these things without major capital outlay. (*Canadian Hotel and Restaurant Journal* September 15, 1955:23)

When Statistics Canada started collecting information, in 1953, on "food away from home" as part of the "urban family's food expenditure," 9.9 percent of the average food budget in urban areas was spent away from home; this figure has now tripled. The marketing strategy of luring the family away from a home-cooked meal to a fast-food restaurant involves selling the idea that this does not mean that the woman is not fulfilling her responsibilities as a homemaker. Indeed, the large fast-food chains are careful to present their product as wholesome and as part of the "American Way of Life." As married women with families took on wage labour, the family would be more likely to eat supper out. The away-from-home percentage of the food budget is the highest when the wife is a fulltime wage earner (Statistics Canada 1984).

As the restaurant business attempted to create new markets for the abundant goods and services produced, the relationship between the domestic economy and wage work changed: a lucrative and expansive market was discovered inside the family, changing the nature of domestic work (Ewen 1980). Caring for one's family became "consumption work," carried out in shopping malls and service centres. Increased competition, however, was organized to increase the profit margins of the seller, not the convenience of the consumer (Weinbaum and Bridges 1979).

All members of the family, from young children to aging grandparents, are the targets of a variety of marketing strategies geared toward increasing consumption. The teen market, in 1991, was worth an estimated six billion dollars and predictions are that it will be worth ten billion dollars within a decade (Strauss 1991). This pressure to buy means that women and their teenaged sons and daughters need and want wages. While all members of a working-class family have always had to participate in the struggle to survive, the difference now is that there is more need. This general process of encouraging the creation of a market can be documented for the restaurant industry specifically.

New Work Opportunities in the Fast-Food Industry

By the 1980s, most women and young people in Canada had paid jobs. In 1986, more than seven out of every ten women in Canada between the ages of fifteen and forty-five were in the labour force. Women and young people form a disproportionate number of the low-wage earners in insecure minimum-wage employment (Census of Canada 1986). The 1986 Census of Canada findings were that women were almost twice as likely as men to be working for $4 an hour or less. Forty percent of low-wage earners were young people between the ages of sixteen and nineteen, and another 24 percent were under twenty-four years of age. The "disappearing middle" in work opportunities has been described in a number of studies for the Economic Council of Canada (1990) and Statistics Canada.[4] While some new jobs in the service industry pay quite well (computer programming or systems design, for example), most of the new entrants for the labour force are ending up in service jobs earning substantially less in 1986 than their counterparts had in 1981 (Myles, Picot, and Wannell 1988). Given the loss of so many manufacturing jobs in Canada in the early 1990s, the situation for new job holders has become even more serious.

In this economic environment, as "good jobs" disappear, more and more workers are finding their options limited to minimum-wage, part-time employment, such as is found in the fast-food industry. Thus, rather than being a job for temporary workers who don't consider their wage employment to be their primary obligation, fast-food jobs are now often the only type of employment available.

In an attempt to explore the working conditions of fast-food workers, I worked in a Burger King outlet in Mississauga, Ontario, in the early 1980s for five months and again briefly, in the summer of 1988, in downtown Toronto. Burger King was owned at that time by the Pillsbury Corporation and was subsequently taken over by an even larger conglomerate, the London-based Grand Met PFC. Burger King is ranked number two internationally in fast-food companies and the work is organized in a way that is very similar to McDonald's. In 1978, Donald Smith, the former head of operations at McDonald's, became president of Burger King in order to implement the same work system that he had developed for his previous company.

The development of small microprocessor chips allowed electronic cash registers to be linked to an in-store computer that collected information on unit levels. As electronic cash registers were introduced into the larger chains in the 1970s (McDonald's and Burger King), it became possible to plan staffing needs according to hourly sales projections. Not only could unskilled workers be productively employed, they could be deployed to further minimize the costs of their labour, by making sure the minimum number of workers were hired to do the maximum amount of work. This social organization of work was determined through centrally organized simulation studies that took place in the headquarters of the parent company: Miami for Burger King and Chicago for McDonald's.

As the customer looks into the open kitchen of a McDonald's or a Burger King outlet, it is not only the walls between the serving areas and the food assembly that have disappeared. The restaurant chef has been eliminated in a fast-food outlet along with the pots and pans. The fries, for example, arrive frozen, pre-cut, and in plastic bags. Each work motion is specified in a manual issued by head office that describes how the fries are to be removed from these bags and placed in a fry basket, ready to be prepared. Nothing is left to chance—or the discretion of the worker.

The fries are cooked in a computer-controlled fry vat and then emptied into the bagging station. A special scoop has been designed for the bagging procedures that can control the portion of each bag of fries. Every part of the bagging process is described in minute detail in the Burger King manual: how to pick up the scoop, how to hold the bags, how to scoop up the fries. Each move in the preparation of fries has also been timed: seven seconds are allotted to placing the fry basket in the fry pot, thirteen seconds to dumping the fries into the bagging station and returning the basket to the holding rack, five seconds to filling the first bag in the bagging cycle, and three seconds to packing each subsequent bag. The worker operates a computerized cooking machine that performs the necessary operations. The labour process is designed so that virtually any unskilled body with sufficient energy could be trained to do any required job in food production. This process, however, has not been fully automated since it is cheaper for this industry to remain labour intensive as long as unskilled workers can be used. Because of the fluctuating demand for restaurant meals in the course of the day, it is more economical to use minimum-wage workers who, unlike expensive machinery, can be sent home when demand falls.

Marketing the Smile

A labour process has been developed that uses untrained workers as "machine tenders," plugging them into a system or food assembly that gives them virtually no discretion in the work process. The large fast-food outlets have found this workforce can be used not only as cheap intensive labour, but also to help sell the food. However, the insistence that workers adopt suitable attitudes to help sell a meal also acts as a way of ensuring acquiescence to an unusually rigid and stressful organization of work.

Adapting the task breakdown and systematized operation from a manufacturing to a service setting was an innovative breakthrough for the industry, and in this, McDonald's took the lead. However, they did not stop there. In what Arlie Hochschild called the "managed heart" (Hochschild 1983), fast-food companies attempted to harness the human feelings of their employees for a dual purpose. On the one hand, it was a good way to expand the market, and on the other hand, it proved to be a very effective technique to monitor workers' acquiescence.

Since the post-World War Two expansion, the restaurant industry has been aware of the need to simulate a family-type setting if customers are to be lured out of their homes and into the market.[5] As early as the 1950s, the industry warned just how difficult a challenge this could be. Competing with the woman at home is no easy task because she "puts love into her cooking" (*Canadian Hotel and Restaurant Journal* 1955). The industry uses a labour force lured away from nonwaged activities in the home and available for bargain prices. Women and young people can be trained to produce a friendly, welcoming setting for fast-food patrons. The employees are told to think of customers as "guests." Doing the job well means not just quickly serving people the food they order, but making them "happy." Employees are told:

> Your job is a sort of social occasion. You meet people, you want these people to like you, to like visiting your restaurant. (Burger King handout n.d.)

Part of this attempt to simulate a non-market setting is to adopt the characteristics of a real person, while obliterating any variation in what these re-created persons actually do or say. While the worker must perform exactly according to specifications laid down in Burger King headquarters in Miami, she/he is nevertheless required to appear as if she/he were an individual. This is accomplished by means of a name tag with the employee's first name on it. This identification of a crew member as an individual is thought to be important both for crew morale and for the customer:

> Guests like to think of you as a person, not some sort of robot. Knowing your first name helps them be friendly towards you. That's why you make sure your name tag is on—straight, with the safety catch fastened, before you greet your first guest of the day. (Burger King handout n.d.)

There is an attempt to erode the distinction between eating at home and eating out for the consumer. Management asks workers to ignore the distinction between being a paid employee at Burger King and one's personal life. Employees are encouraged to look good, just as they would on other social occasions:

> Know how you have more fun at parties and on dates when you're

sure you look your best? Same thing goes at your job. Except maybe its more important to look great—because you're meeting more people. (Burger King handout n.d.)

The training of Burger King crew members is planned at Burger King University in Miami, where managers are given courses on how to handle their workforce. Much of the curriculum consists of imparting what the Burger King University calls "people skills." The idea is to teach their workforce to do things "not well, but right." The women workers are thought to be easier to deal with, as they have fewer options and so will be more reliable workers. As one ex-manager put it:

Let's face it—what other kind of jobs are available? Where else can they go—to a variety store? They have responsibilities to their kids, want to see them off to school and be there for them when they get home from school at night and want to be looked after. The job at Burger King gives them a bit of extra money. They live nearby and even if the job isn't too pleasant, it'll do. (Interview: ex manager, Burger King outlet)

The young people can present more of a challenge:

Let's think of, say, a Roman ship that's being rowed by galley slaves on its way to war. You want them to work hard, your business needs them to work hard. How do you get them to smile? It's hard—after all, the work is rush, rush, rush, clean, clean, clean. Having those kids lined up begging to work. How do they do it? (Interview: ex manager, Burger King outlet)

There is a tremendous emphasis on having what the company calls the "right attitude." Indeed, managers informed me that an improper attitude was *the* most common reason for being "let go." I was chastized for having a "bad attitude." Challenging any of the directives of the managers, no matter how contradictory or confusing, along with insufficient smiling, indicates that the worker might be a "bad apple," and could ruin the whole barrel (or morale in the entire outlet).[6] For an industry that spends a great deal of time and energy on preventing unionization, the presence of "bad apples" can have serious consequences. A good, positive attitude that will reflect "feelings for the job, Burger King, their fellow workers, and their superiors" (Burger King handout n.d.) is essential. Smiling is part of how one displays a "good attitude," particularly if the employee is working at the cash register where customer contact is closest. A handout for Burger

King counter workers contained the following instructions:

> Smile with a greeting and make a positive first impression. Show
> them you are "GLAD TO SEE THEM." Include eye contact with
> the cheerful greeting. (Burger King handout n.d.)

> When the customer feels and sees a good attitude, they sense
> concern for them and their needs. This then presents one reason
> for their liking for Burger King and ultimately they return. An
> excellent employee attitude will be pleasant, cheerful, smiling
> and courteous at all times with customers, fellow workers and
> supervisors. They should show obvious pride in work and em-
> ployment. (Burger King handout n.d)

In a service industry, such as Burger King, the common interests of
the management and crews are stressed through cooperation to provide
better customer service. However, motivating crew to work as hard as
they can to please the customer does not improve the wages of the
workers, but it does help Burger King's sales and profits.

The Burger King Workers

The Burger King in which I worked was a fairly large outlet, located in
a shopping mall. Management tried to maintain a crew of about a hundred
workers, although this figure fluctuated. Approximately 75 percent of the
workers were young teenagers, with an average age of sixteen years,
although sometimes workers as young as fourteen were hired. They were
evenly divided between young men and women. This group would staff
the restaurant on evenings and weekends during the school months. When
the restaurant was busy, twenty to twenty-five people would be working
at any one time.

During the daytime, members of the crew were predominantly
"older" married women. (Although I refer to the married women as
"older," their average age I would estimate to be under thirty years.) There
was also a sprinkling of younger women who had dropped out of high
school, and for short periods, a few young men in the same situation.
There was one head manager, one first assistant, two second assistants,
and three swing managers. The people who made up this group changed
constantly as head management policy was to move them from store to
store. These were young men and women in their late teens and early
twenties, with young men in the majority. They were expected to work
different shifts, weekends, and overtime with no extra pay. Some of the
crew members, about eight in all, were "production leaders." They were

paid an hourly wage only a few cents higher than the crew, most of whom were paid minimum wage.

Why would people take a job at Burger King? Most of the married women had little formal education. They were women with working-class husbands, and they were working to make ends meet. Many of them kept their money separately to spend as they saw fit. One young woman who was pregnant was working for what she termed "extras." She wanted to buy a baby carriage for her new baby. The women with families who worked in the daytime took the job for reasons that had little to do with the actual work. As one woman said:

> It was a job, and it was steady and it was close. I could ride my bike to work. They were actually fairly good with me about the hours they would give me.

Another woman explained:

> With this job, I could be home when the kids returned from school. Babysitting is so expensive that it really doesn't pay to get a fulltime job.

Paid work with other people around was experienced as a relief from the monotony of being home alone. One woman explained that she felt very depressed at home. She enjoyed working, because of the change in surroundings:

> I go home and I come here. It's not just the money because the money is not enough. It's like living in two worlds.

The daytime older workers would arrive early to sit in the crew room, have a cup of coffee, and chat. The crew room was in the basement of the restaurant—a small oblong room, most of which was taken up by a large table surrounded by benches. Crew members would sit around the table before or after shifts. As well, in the daytime, a few workers had long enough shifts to warrant a break. The lives of many of the women who worked at Burger King were tiring. All the women that I met did all their family's housework and childcare, except for one woman, whose twelve-year-old daughter would help clean and make supper. It seemed that the women had no power to insist on more help from their husbands. Indeed, they felt fortunate to have husbands at all. One afternoon, the subject in the crew room was why brides cry on their wedding day. "Out of relief that they've found a husband," said one woman.

While working conditions at Burger King were not particularly desirable, in some ways they were better than those that prevailed at home. As one woman with two children at home put it:

> At least when I come here, I'm recognized. If I do a good job, a manager will say something. Here I feel like a person. I'm sociable and I like being amongst people. At home I'm always cleaning up after everybody and nobody ever notices.

I became friends with a young woman who had left school after grade ten. When I met her, she had two children and a jealous husband. He would disappear as often as he could to go hunting with his friends and rarely took his family anywhere. She felt her options to be very limited. The choices she had were remaining within a not very happy marriage, which at least provided her with an apartment, food, and clothing or going on welfare. She felt that she couldn't find a job that paid enough to support herself and her children. So she had decided to stay in the marriage. For her, like other women, getting out of the house and meeting new people was one of the big advantages of coming to work.

The conversations among the women in the crew room were rarely about work, unless some particularly noteworthy incident had occurred.[7] Most often the discussion would revolve around marriages, husbands, and children or decorating the house. For the women with families, the ties that they developed with their co-workers had to do with the shared commonalities of home life, rather than their shared paid workplace.

On evenings and weekends, the store was staffed by a fairly even balance of teenaged boys and girls still attending school. They came from a variety of ethnic backgrounds, including Jamaican, Chinese, Portuguese, Italian, and Turkish. The economic circumstances of the families of these young workers varied, but the majority were free to use the money they earned as they pleased: to buy clothing, eat out, or go to discos. But a few were directly helping to support their families. As the economic situation in Canada worsens, it is likely that more families will rely on wages earned by their young people. Like the daytime workers, the teenagers took advantage of the socializing opportunities in the crew room. There was a great deal of joking, flirting, food fights in various forms, and beauty sessions—one of the workers was an expert in making French braids and another in applying make-up. Young men and women talked about school tests, weekend plans, clothes, new cassette tapes. As hiring was done locally, many of the crew members went to the same school, and this provided some common ground for how they related to one another.

Workers' feelings about their jobs changed with time. The younger workers when they first started work would be terribly enthusiastic about having a job and earning their own money. For most of them, it was their first job, and the experience promised to be fun. However, the scheduling system at Burger King took tremendous advantage of a teenager's situation. Students were expected to make themselves available to work for a maximum number of hours with no guarantees about when they might be called. Each week, the outlet manager posted the list of workers and shifts for the coming week. People were expected to come to work with little advance notice and at irregular hours. Sometimes, if the store was busy, a manager would call up a young person to come earlier than the scheduled time. On the other hand, if it was slow, people would be asked to leave. The Burger King workforce was expected to display a work ethic that would lead them to place responsibilities to Burger King above everything else in their lives: school, family, and friends. No firm scheduling commitments were made to the older, daytime women workers either, but in practice it was not feasible to schedule them in quite as arbitrary a manner as the teenagers. Thus the married women generally were assigned work during school hours, with a more or less regular schedule from week to week.

The dividing line between those who were called "fulltime " and "part-time" workers (that is, those who worked regularly during school hours and those scheduled on evenings and weekends) also seemed to demarcate different social groups. During holidays and in the summer, the two groups mixed, as older and younger workers were scheduled together. However, overall it was age and circumstance (students in high school, housewives with young children) rather than class, gender, or ethnicity that provided the sense of commonality among workers.

In the crew room, I saw young teenagers of all ethnic and racial groups joking and teasing each other. Management, on the other hand, sometimes expressed racist attitudes towards the workers. One young woman I spoke to just after she had quit told me that she was fed up with the job, and besides, one of the managers called her a "nigger." Later, I asked a young Black man if this ever happened to him. He told me that one of the managers routinely called him "Sambo," and this act of blatant racism was confirmed by his two brothers. When I asked why they hadn't complained, as this is hardly Burger King policy, not to mention contrary to provincial human rights laws, one of the brothers explained that if he wanted the job, the best course of action was to do nothing and "not to make waves." The message that Burger King conveyed is that it doesn't matter what the issue is, or how your dignity is assailed, challenging the hierarchy is not acceptable.

Conclusion

The fast-food industry has perfected a model of a tightly controlled and monitored organization of production where any real input from workers is actively discouraged. It has successfully thwarted most unionizing attempts in North America by a process of encouraging workers' contributions to a "team" in a collectivity that is defined by and through management. In recent years, we have heard much about the application of the "team concept" or Japanese-style management techniques that supposedly challenge Fordist forms of worker organization, drawing upon workers' knowledge and experience to increase productivity. While the fast-food example is much more blatant in the way that managerial prerogatives are exercised, there is a good deal of evidence that North American workers who have lived with the "team concept" have found it only a slightly different path to an end that is the same as that of the fast-food industry, i.e., developing new, more sophisticated forms of intensifying work and increasing productivity (Slaughter and Parker 1991; Hadley forthcoming; Robertson, Rhinehart, Huxley et al. 1992).

While not concerned with providing conditions such as decent pay and benefits that will prevent high turnover, the fast-food industry utilizes an ideology of familism to erode the distinction between workers' jobs and the interest of the company. A parody of a non-commercial setting is invoked and, for their minimum wage, workers are expected to be "individuals": to act in a friendly manner, smile, and make their customers feel like guests. However, these "feelings" are as strictly monitored as are the steps in making a Whopper (a large Burger King hamburger). The greetings for the customer are variants of a script designed in Head Office. Personal interaction must not interfere with "SOS" or "Speed of Service." These considerations shape the daily operation of Burger King.

Marketing food that even the industry admits is quite mediocre involves convincing customers that the "dining experience" proffered by eating fast-food will provide the promise of leisure. Diners are told in a McDonald's jingle: "Give yourself a break today," while Burger King claims: "We do it your way." If women are tired because of the work that they do, then individually they can hope to buy their way to a better life through the market, without the "sweat and grime of social change" (Jacoby 1975). The international expansion in fast-food preaches essentially the same message. Private enterprise and the development of profitable corporations are touted as "making things better" for people everywhere, from Central America to the former Soviet Union.

As privatization, deregulation, and the rule of the "bottom line" deplete the resources available to the public sector in Canada, we see private, fast-food companies moving in to fill the gap. Presenting and perhaps sincerely believing themselves to be charitable and community-minded citizens, fast-food companies find lucrative markets in the schools, hospitals, and other publicly-funded resources such as zoos and sports arenas. For example, marketing gimmicks such as the Pizza Hut and McDonald's literacy programs reward first graders with fast-food gift certificates, simultaneously helping to promote their product, as well as a benign image.

While the marketing image may be benign, the effects of the growth of the fast-food industry have not been healthy from the point of view of ecological concerns or feeding people in countries that are sources of meat for the North American hamburger. One of the demands for entry into the International Monetary Fund is restructuring, with an emphasis placed on an export-oriented economy. As the fast-food industry mushroomed in size in the 1970s, the U.S. began to import beef in large quantities, fostering cattle ranching in tropical Latin America to produce cheap beef for the American market. By the mid-1970s, two thirds of Central America's arable land was in cattle production, while local consumption of beef decreased. Rain forests are still destroyed to make room for cattle ranches. And the ability of local peasants to produce sufficient protein in traditional foods, such as beans, to sustain themselves has been reduced. The end result is that the average domestic cat in the U.S. now consumes more beef than the average Central American person (Skinner 1985).

The fast-food companies sell themselves as family restaurants, using family members to serve the food, and family values to control their workforce and to attract families to eat there. However, as we learn more about what happens inside many family households, we begin to look at the analogy in a different light. The work situation in a fast-food outlet is all too reminiscent of the lack of control women and young people have inside patriarchal, authoritarian families. While families are supposed to be tied together by a mutual desire to nurture and care for each other, we know that those who have power in families can often use it to damage and exploit weaker members.[8] Image and illusion permeate the industry. We need to find methods of weaving family, community, and workplace together in very different, non-exploitative ways. Perhaps in Canada, an exploration of the efforts that people have made in other parts of the world will help us to learn the meaning of resistance and to understand what the notion of a true collectivity involves. An education in new forms of organizing under difficult conditions can be a different kind of North American import from some Third World countries and one that can benefit all of us.

Notes

1. I am thinking of the economic embargo and U.S. aid to the contras which influenced the outcome of the Nicaraguan elections in 1990, and also the general policies dictated by the International Monetary Fund. Many analysts believe that the attempt of the U.S. to control world oil prices was an important factor in the war against Iraq.
2. When *Advertising Age* produced a list in "What's Hot on T.V. Worldwide," *Dynasty* was one of the top favourites for the Third World (Sklair 1991:151).
3. See Reiter (1991) for a fuller development of this argument. References include a variety of census figures on the restaurant industry, as well as personal interviews.
4. See also Myles, Picot and Wannell (1988).
5. A review of the articles on marketing, in the restaurant industry papers, the *Canadian Hotel and Restaurant Journal,* the *Foodservice and Hospitality Magazine,* the *Nation's Restaurant News,* and the marketing techniques used by these companies, shows how the child in the family is targeted. See Reiter (1991).
6. The head manager of the store explained this to me, using this term.
7. For example, when a head office representative arrived unexpectedly to check up on service; or as happened once, when a crew member was attacked while asking rowdy customers to leave.
8. Abuse in the family is far more common than we had previously thought and figures for child and wife abuse support this argument, as does the discrepancy between the hours women and men devote to domestic labour.

CHAPTER SEVEN

DOMESTIC LABOUR IN THE RETAIL SECTOR: DEPARTMENT STORE WORK

Patricia C. McDermott

You can't blame the public because they go in the stores and they see someone who is fairly well-dressed, who is calm and cool . . . and they think that is what they do—walk around with long nails. If it was like that we'd be overpaid. That's the surface . . . selling the stuff is about ten percent.

This paper is about the invisible skills, responsibilities and effort involved in retail work in large department stores. On close examination it becomes clear that this type of work is classically undervalued women's work. Furthermore, the division of labour within a large department store is directly related to employment inequity as well as discriminatory pay for female department store workers.

For decades, retailing corporations have paid rock-bottom wages for this female-dominated service work which historically has been at the heart of often huge profits. The team work and attention to thousands of small details that result in the smooth functioning of store departments, the product knowledge and sales skills that translate into repeat customers, and the quite surprising amount of strenuous physical labour involved in this type of retail work have all gone largely unacknowledged and underpaid. Along with a basic undervaluation of the work of much female-dominated retail work, the distinction between commissioned sales staff and salaried retail clerks underlies a staggering wage differential (over 100 percent) and provides retail giants with a sizable pool of male "salesmen" from which to recruit managers for the upper levels of the organization. The system of having largely female salaried sales clerks and predominantly male commissioned sales personnel is interesting in that they do virtually the same work. The difference is that, as one retail worker noted ironically,

... well the men sell so-called "big ticket items" like refrigerators, stoves and furniture—things that women don't know anything about. While the women sell almost everything else—including snow blowers, lawn mowers and power tools.

This portrait of retail work is drawn from fifty tape-recorded interviews conducted—in keeping with the female-dominated character of this sector—primarily with women (forty-three of fifty interviews). In this chapter we refer primarily to the interviews with women. The discussions about their work took approximately thirty to forty minutes and were responses to the question, "Tell me about your work." The conversations were shaped by appropriate prompting questions about how long they had worked in their departments, how the work was done, and so on.[1]

Most of those interviewed were married with children. On the whole they were in families in which their relatively low incomes represented a major part of the family budget. About two-thirds of their spouses (or parents in the case of those living at home) held "working-class" jobs like streetcar drivers, mechanics, auto workers, and in a few cases they too worked as sales clerks. About one-third of the spouses/parents were economically "middle class" and were accountants, high school teachers, and middle-level managers. They ranged in age from twenty-five to sixty-seven, although most of those interviewed were between thirty-five and fifty. The majority had completed four or five years of high school, and two-thirds of those interviewed had children still at home. Many said they were attracted to retail work because it was "close to home" and offered flexible hours more conducive to family life than a nine-to-five job in an office. About half of those interviewed, however, said that they would have liked to do office work, but as one typical respondent noted: "I ended up in retail because I couldn't type." The highly gender-based segmented labour market, with its characteristically limited range of jobs "appropriate for women," clearly provides a vast workforce for service sector work such as retail.

In keeping with the traditional and current profile of Canadian department store retail workers, a majority of those interviewed were white and tended to be born in Canada. It should also be noted that most of the interviewees were so-called "regular part-time," a group of long-term employees who work from twenty-two to thirty-two hours a week. The growth of this type of workforce is typical of the retail sector in Canada, as cost-cutting retail organizations move to a more "flexible" workforce and favour part-time over full-time employees. In fact, interviewees at each of the outlets mentioned that their store had hired no full-time employees for at least four to five years. The "section head" position—a supervisor who runs a store department—is typically a full-time one and is usually a person promoted from the regular part-time ranks.

The interviewing was undertaken from June to December 1985, immediately following a five and a half month strike at six southern Ontario locations of Eaton's, one of Canada's largest department store chains.[2] This is significant in that the strike caused these workers to confront many commonly-held misconceptions about the nature of their work. Many of those interviewed recounted experiences in which unsupportive members of the public passing their picket line would make comments to them that suggested that, "minimum wage is okay for someone who just stands there at the cash register and smiles," or that, "anyone could do your work." Even a mayor of North York, a city north of Toronto, publicly stated that in his opinion the strikers were lazy. The public outcry that his comments created resulted in his having to work in an outlet of The Bay department store for one day, as one striker put it, "to make up—as sort of an election gimmick." He eventually admitted that, "there was more to it than I thought." Derogatory comments about their work led to a degree of indignation which benefited this research greatly. When asked to describe their work many felt they were responding to the misunderstanding that they believed many people had about what they did for a living. As one frustrated woman commented: "For God's sake, put that in your book—we work like Trojans—and nobody seems to know about it!"

"Retail work is first and foremost hard work"

When many of the interviewees were describing their jobs the conversation often led to the people with which they worked most closely in their departments. They were typically complimentary about their "team" and frequently described them as, "believing in a hard day's work" or as someone, "who likes to go home knowing they've earned their pay." The two overall impressions that the interviews give about retail work are that, not only is it far more complex than is commonly thought, it is also a great deal more physically demanding work than people who have never done retail work assume.

About fifteen to twenty years ago Eaton's had a system of "stock boys" to help out in most departments. Over the years the number of stockroom workers has greatly diminished to the point where they are now only readily available in a handful of departments—for example, furniture and appliances —interestingly in the male-dominated "commissioned sales" areas. Many people said the stockroom workers were never around when you needed them and, "If you try to call one to your own department, it takes an hour or two." Indeed they were often unavailable when customers asked for help to their cars with heavy items.

The back-breaking aspects of their work were vividly described by numerous respondents. Here are two typical examples which not only capture the emphasis on heavy work but also stress how those interviewed felt their work is not understood.

> I guess a lot of people think that behind the scenes there's all these people busy opening crates and unloading things. They have no idea it's us. . . . I can't think of a department where the work isn't heavy. Even in Sheets and Blankets—I mean they come in huge boxes. Candy is hard work—even in Cosmetics they get big crates of the packages of perfume and lipstick coming in.

> When I go home I even used to have to explain it to my mother. I'd say, "Boy am I tired," and she'd say, "Why, what did you do?" So I'd say, "Mom I have a sale to get out. I had to lug fifty boxes out of the stockroom, hang up all the clothes, move around fixtures." I mean—it's hard work!

Not only is retail work far more physically demanding than most people think, it is also often hazardous. One woman who worked in the Babies Wear department described skids coming into her section from shipping with fifteen to twenty cribs on them, each weighing about fifty pounds. The cribs have to be hauled off the skid and dragged, "maybe a hundred feet and stacked along the wall at the back of the stockroom." She has had tendonitis twice and had to have cortisone shots. Another describes helping "a nice elderly gentleman" with a power saw out to his car; she injured her back "and was flat for three months." One interviewee commented that potting soil was her problem. "I see potting soil come in and my back starts hurting." Another said that she remembers she wanted a "respectable" job in retail to "avoid the work hazards of a factory job," a setting in which her husband had been hurt twice. She found it ironic that she ended up in hospital after severely straining her shoulder muscles while pulling a large box of crystal out onto the floor. Remembering the day she "was carried out of work," she said she joked with her supervisor: "Now I know why they call it 'lead crystal.'"

Besides the strenuous physical exertion involved in moving heavy merchandise, the interviews contained numerous stories about how people had cut, burned, and bruised themselves while setting up demonstration power and sports equipment, cribs, high chairs, barbecues, sewing machines, shelving units, fireplace screens, lawn mowers, and snow blowers. One woman recounts how a huge pile of Cabbage Patch dolls fell on her when a large shelf in a stock room collapsed. "Now you wouldn't think dolls would be heavy . . . try four or five hundred of them." She was off work for two months.

The dust and fumes present in the stock rooms and basement storage areas, as well as poorly lit and dangerous back stairs, were also often mentioned as contributing to poor working conditions. One interviewee succinctly described the "basic broken container" problem that frequently made their worksites unpleasant: "Anything can pour out, stink up the place and make a mess—cleaning chemicals, paint, lighter fluid, even bath salts, perfume, and shoe polish in certain quantities can be very offensive, make you cough, wreck your clothes."

"We are not unskilled workers"

> Retail work is also complex work that you get better and better at over the years. . . . To be a good sales clerk in a department store like Eaton's you can't just walk in off the street and do a good job. It takes training and experience. Now I'm not talking about people who say, "I just work here lady."

Like the general misconception that work in department stores is clean, safe, and involves little physical exertion, consumers are usually not aware of the skills involved in running a section of a large department store. Most of those interviewed took offence at the suggestion that their work was "easy," "unskilled," and done by anyone "off the street." One woman from the Scarborough Town Eaton's store describes an interaction she had at a Christmas party attended by the comparatively better paid, largely male Liquor Board Workers, a union to which her boyfriend belonged. She remembers one man saying that he did not think she should earn more than four or five dollars an hour, "for what you do." She was furious and her reply was surely a classic:

> How can you say that? You think you deserve to earn more? You don't even know half of what I know. All you do is shuffle bottles around all day, and look at what you've got, the benefits your union has won for you. Don't tell me what I deserve and don't deserve. We work twice as hard as you. I have to know more than you.

For those who take on the responsibility for the operation of a department, the job demands the coordination of many tasks to keep the department in what was often referred to as, "smooth working order." The "section heads," who could be described as first-line supervisors, responsible for the efficient functioning of a department, are typically assisted by a small number of regular part-timers who share in the organization of the department as a whole. The "team work" was repeatedly emphasized throughout the interviews. For example, Betty from Eaton's Shoppers World store remarked that, "Ruby and I took over Shoes and really got it in top running order," while Bernice from the Scarborough Town store noted that you have to work well with your co-workers or, "things just don't get done." Whether it's moving merchandise or organizing sales, "You become a little team." The "team concept" is currently a prominent theme in many "modern" management techniques; retail workers in large department stores could provide a good illustration of how this approach has worked for years.

Coordination efforts were heavily focused on keeping a stock room clean, neat, and organized so merchandise could be efficiently stored and easily retrieved when a customer asked for something. As one interviewee who worked in the Luggage department noted: "You can't say, 'Well, I'll see if we have one in the stock' and then be gone for five minutes." Christmas and back-to-school sales as well as seasonal clothes and equipment means that merchandise always comes in months ahead of time and has to be "squeezed in somewhere" until it is sold over a relatively short period. Many described the stock room as a place, "where you can hardly turn around," and ". . . overflowing, simply overflowing." As a woman who had worked in the Linens department for sixteen years stressed:

> The heart of a successful "White Sale" is a stock room in tip top shape. If you can't get it out to the floor when people want it, it's not gonna sell. I feel organizing that stock room, making it function properly, is a big part of my job.

To convey a sense of what retail work is like for those who help run the departments in which they work, in the pages that follow the comments of two co-workers from Cosmetics and three from Hardware are used to describe the operation of a department. These descriptions not only demonstrate the degree of coordination needed to run a department, but they also give a sense of the broad scope of often complex, and again strenuous, work duties for which these women were responsible. For example, there are many discussions, especially from the "section heads," about an incredible amount of paperwork that has to be done. Books had to be kept up to date, accounts and sales reports submitted, and schedules created. It seems that some of the paperwork was done on the employee's own time. Several interviewees who had specifically avoided office work because they could not type, said that it was ironic that they ended up in a job where they had to do so much paperwork: "It was like being in an office."

In discussions of their work we also hear about the vast "product knowledge" that so many of those interviewed possess—the kind of knowledge that creates regular customers and the kind of knowledge that many of those interviewed regretted that Eaton's was increasingly trying to do without. As one noted, "Eaton's is becoming just like one of those stores where the sales help don't even know where anything is—let alone how it works." In many ways, as we shall see, these are descriptions of retail sales work, "the way it should be," as one interviewee said, "You know—where the sales clerk is courteous, knowledgable, and helpful."

It was clear that these women have a keen sense of what constitutes "good service" and what was frequently referred to as "the art of selling." Good service means not letting the customer know that Eaton's no longer has a carry-out service, but instead offering to help the customer out to their car with the merchandise. It also means not disappearing into a stock room for lengthy periods while a customer is waiting. Good sales skills involve learning how to deal with people and not pressuring customers or selling them things they do not need. Many of those interviewed spoke of the care they took in making sure that the information about the product was correct and the merchandise itself was not inappropriate or possibly even harmful. For example, Betty from the Scarborough Town store mentioned how she felt responsible when she sold baby shoes:

> You know the first pair of shoes are very important . . . a child can say, "this hurts" but a baby can't. And young mothers have no idea, they rely on you.

Claudia, who worked in the Ladies Wear at the Yonge-Eglinton store, described how she was careful about giving information to customers about the care of the clothing they are buying. She said that people often ask her whether they can wash items with "dry clean only" tags on them:

> I can't just answer, "Oh sure you can wash it," just to make the sale. . . . You have to give detailed, explicit instructions. "Wash it by hand, warm water and mild soap. Then rinse in cold water and let it hang to dry. Don't wring it out—just let it drip dry. The fabric is very delicate. And use a plastic hanger.". . . You've got

119

to be careful or you end up with someone bringing back a wrecked blouse and saying, "*You* said I could wash it."

The first description of a department is based on three interviews with women in the Hardware department at Eaton's Scarborough Town store. Sheila and Val were regular part-time, while Ruth was a fulltime section head. All are mothers, were in their forties when interviewed, and had worked for Eaton's for eleven, thirteen, and fifteen years respectively.

Hardware

Ruth, Sheila, and Val all emphasized the physical work that had to be done in their department. As Ruth noted, "We cart stuff around, big, huge, heavy barbecues, power tools—you name it. We regularly put out five hundred gallons of paint.... We put together power saws and move them, table saws, shelving units." They described doing what they considered, "extra work, not in my job description," like carrying things out for customers. As Val explains, "Oh yes, I've carried out many a five gallon drum of driveway sealer." Ruth says that helping a customer with carrying has to be done subtly and in an appropriate way for each situation: "If it's a little old lady—no problem. Now if it's a man maybe you'd say, 'It will take too long to get a stockboy. Maybe I could help you with it?' So they wouldn't feel embarrassed."

Sheila comments that running the Hardware department with Ruth and Val is "just like operating a small business." She typically stresses that the three needed to be in constant contact to be "on top of everything." All day long it was: "Watch this and order that. Just keeping track and informing each other of things that needed to be done." Val talked of how they, "learned something new every day," and describes how she taught herself to mix paint to match a little sample brought in by a customer and to help people select the right kind and quantity of wallpaper. Ruth also commented on the product knowledge that the three have built up over the years, like knowing about how power tools work and their safety features and "knowing whether to paint something with this type of paint, whether to use a rust remover."

Sheila was so confident in the sales and organizing skills that she, Ruth, and Val possessed, she developed her own "mythical, revenge scheme" that she had worked out on the picket line while they were on strike. It was a scheme designed to show Eaton's how much they underestimated their work. She fantasized about approaching a competing department store, maybe Simpson's, that had, by her assessment, a hardware section that was in "pretty rough shape." Then "the team" would offer their services "free of charge" to this store and work like crazy until the department was making a certain profit. Then they would steal all the business away from Eaton's and send them regular sales reports to show them where all their business had gone. Although Sheila laughed and said, "Of course, I'm kidding but we could do it I'm sure . . . take a loser and turn it around. We know how to run a top-of-the-line department."

Ruth was the main source of knowledge about new products coming in because she went to information seminars held by Eaton's or the manufacturers and was always careful to bring back extra copies of pamphlets for each of her co-workers and to give them demonstrations about new equipment. As was typical with many of the section heads, Ruth complained about having to attend these product knowledge sessions on her own time. Since she did not drive, she often ended up taking public transportation: "That took hours because they [the sessions] were way out in the West end—Etobicoke, Mississauga."

As the section head, Ruth was also responsible for an incredible amount of paperwork. She did the time sheets and scheduling for the part-timers and students, price changes for sales, sales reports, orders for purchasing, and customer complaints and returns. She talked of how she used to take the scheduling home and then one day decided she was not going to, "ruin one more evening" with it, so she made time for it at work. She did however, still take home something called the, "aged stock" report that had to be done every second month or so:

> You could fill the sheets out in the store but it was hard to enter the information in the books there—too noisy and busy. So I brought it home. It used to take three, even four, nights running—about four hours a night. Now, you didn't get paid for that.

Cosmetics

Together Suzanne and Sue ran the Cosmetics department at Eaton's medium sized Yonge-Eglinton store in downtown Toronto. Sue had worked at Eaton's for five years when she was interviewed, and Suzanne had been with Eaton's for fourteen years, starting as a part-time student while in high school. Both women were in their late twenties when interviewed. Suzanne was single with no children and lived with her parents, while Sue was married and had what she termed the, "dubious distinction" of being the only person pregnant throughout the strike.

Both women talked of the broad array of products they had to know about and keep in stock. Suzanne describes how she was responsible for sixty-two different product lines produced by twenty-eight companies. Within each line there were numerous "sub-lines" which represented hundreds of individual products which had to be regularly counted, ordered, stocked, and returned if damaged or not sold. When she got to work, the first thing she did was open her register. If other people were not on time she opened all four registers. Each opening involves counting "the float" and entering the figures into the appropriate ledger. The next thing she did was tidy her counters and clean all the glass surfaces with a window cleaner. Then she made a list of diminished stock and made her first trip of the day to the stock room. After that she did the daily schedule for the department and began her paperwork. In between sales she did sales reports, accounts, monthly schedules, and, once a month, a report that involves a complete count of all stock. She says this, "can take two or three days because you're always being interrupted: someone is not back from break yet, please authorize this cheque, and so on." On top of all this she has to deal with suppliers who come in and has to be ready to place her orders and make returns. "Then, of course," she noted, "you've got your suppliers coming in without appointments to add a bit to the confusion."

Both Suzanne and Sue felt there was a conflict between how they were supposed to dress and look at the counter and their responsibility for getting merchandise in and out of the stockroom as well as keeping the stockroom organized. Suzanne complained that when you are at the counter your manager wants you to, "look like a million bucks," in make-up, heels, and stockings, but then "haul and tote in the stockroom, going up and down these ladders in your heels, getting runs in your stockings and sweating your make-up off." She describes how a friend of hers was working all day to get out a sale and her supervisor said to her, "You look pale, go put on some lipstick."

Suzanne and Sue both stressed that in a medium-sized store, like the Yonge-Eglinton branch, running a successful Cosmetics counter depended on building up a clientele. People who came in regularly often knew their names and relied on them to have "a special cream they use or a certain lipstick colour in stock." Suzanne insisted that even though her department ran on a "modified" commission system, "I cannot and will not sell something a woman doesn't need—just to make a dollar. . . . You have to be ethical with them or you won't get them back."

Suzanne's knowledge of cosmetics has been built up over the years by reading books, product descriptions and inserts, and especially by attending the courses held by cosmetic companies for retail clerks—again attended on her own time. She kept detailed records of what ingredients were in each product, especially creams and fragrances, in case customers have problems with allergic reactions. Suzanne stressed the importance of keeping their counters well-stocked and the stock room neat and organized. "You can't just doze off for a few days because if the products aren't there—they're not going to sell."

Sue trained to be a cosmetician by taking a two-year course at a community college in Southern Ontario. Not only did the course cover the technical details of how all types of cosmetics are produced, they were also taught selling techniques and about how to work in retail. She was particularly proud of the system they had developed for keeping track of stock and of the fact that sales had improved enormously over the five years she had been in her store. The secret of their success was that if she and Suzanne felt a procedure or routine did not "make sense," they would find a better way to do it:

> For example, we prefer to write out our own sheets. . . . The sheets they gave us to use were impossible. The print was so tiny you just couldn't use it properly. . . . My book for fragrances alone is two or three inches thick.

Clearly Sue and Suzanne worked well together and, like Ruth, Val, and Sheila in Hardware, ran a complex "little business" within their store. The wages for this type of work are some of the lowest in Canada—in the bottom 10 percent of average wages. Yet, a close examination of what is constantly referred to as "unskilled" work reveals that it is work that involves significant skills, effort, and responsibilities that are far beyond the pay and social status accorded to this classic "women's work." One interviewee felt that calling retail work in a department store unskilled was a "myth that saved the employer a lot of money."

"It's Like Housework—Only You Get Paid"

A number of the women compared their work to housework: "It's like running a house," commented Carol, "making purchases, cleaning, dealing with repairmen and all the family dynamics . . . the never-ending picking-up and organizing . . . even cleaning out the garage and the basement. It's all there." In many ways retail work does resemble housework. Retail employers clearly benefit from the transfer of the hidden skills and responsibilities from the domestic sphere to the paid labour market. The attention to detail, the ability to juggle many tasks at once, the social skills involved in dealing with people, all sounded like the running of a household. Many of those interviewed described the "service" aspect of their work as a factor in giving their work a "subservient quality." This was particularly apparent in settings which had bells for customers to ring when there was no sales person at the counter. Although they understood, especially with cutbacks in staff, that the bells were a "necessary evil," almost everyone who had to respond to these bells disliked them. When they discussed their reasons for not wanting to have to respond to customers who were ringing a bell, several mentioned that it put them in "an even more subservient role." As another noted, "It sort of created the idea that 'you are here to serve me.' As a sort of servant."

Face-to-face service is quite common in many areas of women's work in the tertiary sector. Whether in banks, libraries, hotels, restaurants, reception areas, or shops, the "over-the-counter" nature of much service work that women do creates a perception that, as one interviewee noted, "the customer is always right," and as noted above, "You are here to serve me." It generates an expectation of a pleasant, courteous and accommodating service worker, "ready with a smile and," as one worker said, "that hideous expression, 'have a nice day,' that they're always trying to get people to say." Again, the resemblance to housework is strong. Mom is expected to know where everything is, be the family mediator, be pleasant, and serve meals with a smile.

Seeing the parallels between domestic labour and paid service work is important in that, as mentioned above, it allows and encourages a cultural rationale for paying extremely low wages. A retail worker comes to the job with her "innate" domestic skills—"Mom: the chief cook and bottle washer." The skills she has are seen as essentially free—a perception that plays a clear role in the undervaluation of women's work. It also has an impact on the women's perceptions of themselves as workers. Most of those interviewed returned to work after their children were born and many felt quite fortunate and proud of themselves for "landing a job at Eaton's." Quite a number described how they felt when they first got their job, and as one worker typically commented:

> I felt great. Like I'd really accomplished something. I went home and casually said to my husband, "Well I start Monday," and he said, "you're kidding!" . . . I don't know why I was so excited. Probably because Eaton's was considered a "good" employer. Probably because when you've been home with two kids for a few years you can't believe anyone thinks you can do anything else.

Commissioned Sales

As mentioned earlier, the system at Eaton's is essentially one in which the women, the large majority of retail sales personnel, sell most of the merchandise except the "big ticket items," which are sold by a comparatively small group of salesmen who work on a commission system. This approach is similar to that in many department stores in North America. Many reasons for this system were suggested by people who have been in department store retail work for a long time. Several felt that this system has historically been based on the assumption that people, both men and women, preferred to buy major purchases—appliances, furniture, and carpets—from, noted one respondent, "a man dressed in a suit." One interviewee suggested that "years ago" women had to bring their husbands with them to get their approval for the expenditure of a large sum of money, and that: "Men would rather deal with other men when it comes to buying something big. In those days women didn't write big cheques, and of course, they couldn't get credit without their husband's signature." Another respondent's impression was that Eaton's was a very traditional employer and simply wanted to pay men a family wage, "So they put all the men on commission so their wives wouldn't have to work."

Commissioned sales tended to have some form of risk involved whereby if you did not sell a certain amount of merchandise each month you would only make a set wage and would have to sell more the next month before you could start to make your commission. Some of those interviewed felt that most women did not want to take this risk. Others thought that since the commissioned sales system primarily involved fulltime positions many women would not want them because of domestic commitments. Although the flexible hours may initially have been an attractive feature of retail work for many women, at least half of those interviewed who worked "regular part-time" wanted to work more hours. Many wanted at least the maximum allowed in the regular part-time category—thirty-two hours. Most had never thought of "going into commission"—primarily because they did not know what was involved, and most had not known (until the strike) how much more commissioned sales paid. Only one of the respondents had ever applied for a commissioned position and this was someone who had worked on a "modified" commissioned system on a cosmetics counter. This modified system allowed her to make 1 percent of total sales per year. This meant that, in 1985, instead of making the average fulltime salary for a retail clerk at Eaton's of approximately $12,500, she earned about $15,000. In 1985 commissioned salesmen earned on average approximately $28,000.[3]

When those interviewed were asked if they thought they would do a good job in commissioned sales most answered positively. "I can sell jewellery and luggage," commented one respondent, "why wouldn't I be able to sell a dining room set just as well?" Another noted that she thought that:

> In this day and age women could probably sell washing machines and stoves to other women better than men could. . . . After all we're the ones that use these things. We know what features to look for from our own experience. . . . You know, "this tray comes out for easy cleaning"—things like that. After all we're the ones that clean fridges.

Another commented that, "Women seem to have taken over the real estate field. If we sell houses why couldn't we sell furniture just as well?"

A visit to a "big ticket item" area suggests that the department store management does indeed want to project an image of respectability when high priced merchandise is being sold. First of all, the areas tend to be very quiet and there are desks at which discussion and calculations can be made. The salesmen all dress in suits, give customers their business cards, and generally conduct sales in what would be considered a "reserved and professional" manner. No "high pressured salesmen in Eaton's," noted one respondent who "never realized the women were being paid so little until we went on strike."

What is the reason for a system in which the women sell most of the merchandise for so little pay and the men, who do essentially the same work, get paid so much more? Is it that the salesmen actually bring in much more profit to the company, thereby justifying higher pay? Several respondents in commissioned sales suggested this was unlikely given the small size of the commissioned sales departments. Also, it has been rumoured that Eaton's, like many department stores, has been losing money on big ticket items for many years. This is primarily because of intense competition from specialized retailers such as carpet and furniture "warehouse outlets" that have become so popular in the past two decades. Yet the move out of big ticket merchandise has been slow. As mentioned earlier, commissioned sales has historically been a career route to the upper levels of management of the Eaton's corporation itself. Keep the women out of commissioned sales and then there is no possibility of them moving up Eaton's corporate hierarchy. Certainly this system is changing with the approach today of hiring both male and female "management trainees"—"young MBAs" who essentially skip the process of a lengthy apprenticeship on the sales floor. However, the move to this new system again freezes out a group of female employees, many of whom have both motivation and talent for management roles.

A Pay and Employment Equity Approach

Theories of equal pay for work of equal value would suggest that retail work in department stores is classically undervalued female work. A fair, gender-neutral study of their work in comparison with commissioned salesmen reveals a significant undervaluation. Yet, the problem goes deeper. It is also one of employment equity. The separation of these two interrelated issues resulted in the well-known example in the U.S. in which the Equal Opportunities Commission took the retail giant Sears to court because so few women were in commissioned sales. Yet if a combined equal-value employment equity approach were taken, one would ask why women have to leave jobs they do well and enjoy and take male-dominated jobs, when the problem is that their own jobs are undervalued and consequently underpaid?

The Sears example is also unique in that the evolving law in both the U.S. and Canada[4] on "systemic discrimination," which does not require intent on the employer's part, was completely ignored by the court in its decision in Sears' favour. Without the notion of systemic discrimination one is left concluding simply that few women want commissioned sales since only a handful ever applied for these openings. Rather, the question should surely be: how could commissioned sales become integrated? What if Eaton's launched a program to train women sales clerks in the commissioned sales system? Likely many would sign up and eventually decide that they too could try their hand in the "big ticket" world. The attraction of twice as much money alone would clearly operate to entice a sizable number who would want to attempt to sell stoves and furnishings to other women—many of whom surely "in this day and age" do not need their husbands—if they have husbands—along for approval.

The retail case is only one example of many settings in which largely undervalued women's work is located at the bottom of a corporate structure that says, "no women need apply" to the upper echelons of management. Women's work is typically extremely valuable work in terms of profitability of the organization as a whole, and indeed it is often work central to the organization's business. The weavers in the linen and cotton industries, the chambermaids in hotels, the teachers in schools, the librarians in libraries, the tellers in banks, the clerks in the insurance industry, the nurses in hospitals, the sewing machine operators in garment factories, the clerks in shops and department stores—all do work so much at the heart of the business that underpay is clearly directly related to the profitability of enterprises in the private sector or the "cost effectiveness" of public sector employers. Keeping women in low and lower-paid jobs at the bottom of a segregated organizational structure perpetuates the myths that women's wages are secondary to the male's "family wage" and that women are not prepared to make a serious, long-term commitment to paid employment.

The increase in women's labour-force participation, the ever-rising divorce rate, the tendency to smaller family size, and the dramatically increased educational attainment of women, along with some emerging signs of men's willingness to share in the burden of domestic labour, all point to employment structures that must not continue to have segregation and undervaluation as central organizing principles—but instead equal opportunity and fair pay.

Notes

1. This interview data is part of a larger project on the Eaton's strike. See also McDermott 1993:23-43.2.
2. See Pragnell 1989.
3. These estimates were calculated both from the interviewees' responses, some of whom were commissioned salesmen, and from wage data in newspaper reports about the strike.
4. See *Action Travail des Femmes v. CN.* 1985 and *Grigg v. Duke Power* 1974.

REFERENCES

Acker, Joan. "Class, Gender and the Relations of Distribution." *Signs,* 13, 3 (1988): 473-497.

Action Travail des Femmes v. CN Supreme Court Reports, 1985.

Anderson, Grace. "Azoreans in Anglophone Canada." *Canadian Ethnic Studies,* 15 (1983): 73-82.

Arat-Koc, Sedef. "In the Privacy of Our Own Home: Foreign Domestic Workers as Solution to the Crisis in the Domestic Sphere in Canada." *Studies in Political Economy,* 28 (1989): 33n.

____. "Importing Housewives: Non-Citizen Domestic Workers and the Crisis of the Domestic Sphere in Canada." In *Through the Kitchen Window: The Politics of Home and Family.* Edited by M. Luxton, H. Rosenberg and S. Arat-Koc. Toronto: Garamond Press, 1990.

Armstrong, Pat, Jacqueline Choiniere, and Elaine Day. *Vital Signs: Nursing in Transition.* Toronto: Garamond Press, 1993.

Armstrong, Pat, Hugh Armstrong, Patricia Connelly, and Angela Miles. *Feminist Marxism or Marxist Feminism?: A Debate.* Toronto: Garamond Press, 1985.

Barber, Marilyn. "The Women Ontario Welcomed: Immigrant Domestics for Ontario Homes, 1870-1930." In *The Neglected Majority: Essays in Canadian Women's History,* Vol. II. Edited by A. Prentice and S. Trofimenkoff. Toronto: McClelland and Stewart,1985, p. 102n.

Beechey, Veronica. *Unequal Work.* London: Verso, 1987.

Benston, Margaret. *The Political Economy of Women's Liberation.* New York: Monthly Review Press, 1969.

Bernstein, Deborah. "The Subcontracting of Cleaning Work: A Case in the Casualisation of Labour." *The Sociological Review,* 34, 2 (1986): 396-421.

Bhabha, J., F. Klug, and S.Shutter. *Worlds Apart: Women Under Immigration and Nationality Law.* London: Pluto Press, 1985.

Bloch, Harriet. "Changing Domestic Roles Among Polish Women." *Anthropological Quarterly,* 49 (1976): 3-10.

Bose, Christine. "Social Status of the Homemaker." In *Women and Household Labor.* Edited by Sarah Berk. London: Sage Publications, 1980, p. 69n.

Bottomley, Gill, Marie de Lepervanche, and Jeannie Martin. *Intersexions: Gender, Class, Culture and Ethnicity.* Sydney: Allen and Unwin, 1991.

Boyd, Monica. "Immigrant Women: Language, Socioeconomic Inequalities and Policy

Issues." In *Ethnic Demography: Canadian Immigrant Racial and Cultural Variations*. Edited by Shiva S. Halli, Frank Trovato, and Leo Driedger. Ottawa: Carleton University Press, 1990, p. 275-293.

Brand, Dionne. "A Working Paper on Black Women in Toronto: Gender, Race and Class." *Fireweed*, 19 (1984): 26-43.

Bunster, Ximena and Elsa Chaney. *Sellers and Servants: Working Women in Lima Peru*. New York: Praeger Special Studies, 1985.

Burger King. handout, n. d.

Business Week. "Making Yanqui Boodle South of the Border." February 10, 1992, p. 40-43.

Byrne, D. *Waiting for Change: Working in Hotel and Catering*. Low Pay Pamphlet, 42. Published jointly by the Low Pay Unit, London, U.K., and the Hotel and Catering Workers Union, GMBATU, Esher, Surrey, U.K.,1986.

Calliste, Agnes. "Canada's Immigration Policy and Domestics from the Caribbean: The Second Domestic Scheme." In *The Social Basis of Law*, second edition. Edited by Elizabeth Comack and Stephen Brickey. Halifax: Garamond Press, 1991, p. 95n.

Campbell-Platt, K. *Workers in Britain from Selected Foreign Countries: A Briefing Paper*. London: The Runneymede Trust, 1976.

Canada. Economic Council of Canada. *Good Jobs, Bad Jobs: Employment in the Service Economy*. Ottawa, 1990.

___. Employment and Immigration. *Employment Authorizations Issued Abroad Under the Foreign Domestic Movement, January-December 1991, January-December 1992*, unpublished. Ottawa, 1993.

___.Employment and Immigration (Policy Branch). *Foreign Domestic Workers: Preliminary Statistical Highlight Report*. Ottawa, August 1990.

___. Employment and Immigration. *Immigration Manual*. Ottawa.

___. Employment and Immigration. *Live-in Caregiver Program Backgrounder*. Ottawa, 27 April 1992.

___. Employment and Immigration. *Permanent Residents Years of Schooling by Country of Last Permanent Residence for Special Program FDM, January-December 1989*, unpublished. Ottawa, 1991.

___. *Census of Canada. 1986*. Ottawa.

___. Statistics Canada. Cat nos 62-548. Ottawa, 1980.

___. Statistics Canada. Cat nos 62-554. Ottawa, 1984.

___. Statistics Canada. *Women in Canada*, second edition. Ottawa, 1990.

Canadian Child Day Care Federation. *Issues in post-secondary education for quality early childhood care and education*. Ottawa, 1991.

Canadian Hotel and Restaurant Journal. September 15, 1955.

Canadian Union of Postal Workers (CUPW). *Justice for Cleaners*. Toronto, 1987.

Castro, Mary Garcia. "What is Bought and Sold in Domestic Service?" In *Muchachas No More: Household Workers in Latin America and the Caribbean*. Edited by Elsa Chaney and Mary Garcia Castro. Philadelphia: Temple University Press, 1989, p. 105n.

Chaney, Elsa and Maria Garcia Castro, eds. *Muchachas No More: Household Workers in*

Latin America and the Caribbean. Philadelphia: Temple University Press, 1989.

Chaplin, David. "Domestic Service and Industrialization." *Comparative Studies in Sociology.* Edited by Richard Tomasson. vol. 1. Greenwich, CT: JAI, 1978, p. 97-127.

Childcare Resource & Research Unit (in press). *Childcare information sheets: The provinces and territories, 1993.* Toronto: The Childcare Resource & Research Unit, 1993.

Clark-Lewis, Elizabeth. "'This Work had a' End': The Transition from live-in to day work." working paper 2. In *Southern Women: The Intersection of Race, Class and Gender Series.* Memphis: Center for Research on Women, Memphis State University, 1985, p. 21.

Cock, Jacklyn. *Maids and Madams: A Study in the Politics of Exploitation.* Johannesburg: Ravan Press, 1980.

Cohen, Marjorie. *Free Trade and the Future of Women's Work: Manufacturing and Service Industries.* Toronto: Garamond Press, 1987.

___. *Women's Work, Markets, and Economic Development in Nineteenth-Century Ontario.* University of Toronto Press, 1988..

Coley, Soraya Moore. *And Still I Rise: An Exploratory Study of Contemporary Black Private Household Workers.* Ph.D. Dissertation, Bryn Mawr College, 1981.

Coser, Lewis. "Servants: The Obsolescence of an Occupational Role." *Social Forces,* 31 or 52 (1973 or 1974): 52n or 31-40.

Coyle, Angela. "Going Private: The Implications of Privatization for Women's Work. *Feminist Review,* 21 (1985): 5-23.

Dalla Costa, Mariarosa and Selma James. *The Power of Women and the Subversion of the Community.* Bristol: Falling Wall Press, 1972.

DeVan, Mary. *Social, Economic and Political Factors Influencing the Supply and Demand of Foreign Domestic Workers.* Unpublished MA Thesis, University of British Columbia, 1989.

Dill, Bonnie Thornton. *Across the Boundaries of Race and Class: An Exploration of the Relationship Between Work and Family Among Black Female Domestic Servants.* Ph.D. Dissertation, New York University, 1979.

___. "Our Mothers' Grief: Racial Ethnic Women and the Maintenance of Families." *Journal of Family History,* 12, 4 (1988): 415-31.

Doherty, G.*Quality matters in child care.* Huntsville, Ontario: Jesmond Publishing, 1991.

Dronfield, Liz and Paul Soto. *Hardship Hotel.* London: Counter Information Services, 1981.

Elson, Diane. "Market Socialism or Socialization of the Market?" *New Left Review,* 172 (Nov/Dec. 1990).

Elson, Diane and Ruth Pearson. "The Subordination of Women and the Internationalisation of Factory Production." In *Of Marriage and the Market: Women's Subordination in International Perspective.* Edited by Kate Young, Carol Wolkowitz, and Roslyn McCullagh. London: CSE Books, 1990.

Epstein, Rachel. "Domestic Workers: The Experience in B.C." In *Union Sisters.*Edited by

L. Briskin and L. Yan. Toronto: The Women's Press, 1983, p. 222n.

Estable, Alma. *Immigrant Women in Canada: Current Issues.* A background paper prepared for the Canadian Advisory Council on the Status of Women. Ottawa, 1987.

Ewen, Stewart. *Captains of Consciousness.* New York: McGraw Hill, 1980.

Federici, Silvia. "Wages Against Housework." In *The Politics of Housework.* Edited by E. Malos. London: Allison and Busby, 1980.

Financial Post. August 25, 1984.

Finkelstein, B. "Women and the dilemmas of professionalism." in *Professionalism and the Early Childhood Practionner.* Edited by B.Spodek, O.Saracho and D.Peters. Columbia University, New York: Teachers College Press, (1988).

Flavelle, Dana. "The Dilemma Over Domestic Workers." *Toronto Star,* February 1, 1990, p. C5.

Fox, Bonnie. *Hidden in the Household: Women's Domestic Labour Under Capitalism.* Toronto: The Women's Press, 1980.

Freeman, M.D.A. and S. Spencer. *Immigration Control, Blackworkers and the Economy.* Reprinted from the *British Journal of Law and Society*, 6,1(1979): 53-81. University College Cardiff Press.

Friedan, Betty. *The Feminine Mystique.* New York. Dell Publishing, 1963.

Fudge, Judy and Patricia McDermott, eds. *Just Wages: A Feminist Assessment of Pay Equity.* University of Toronto Press,1991.

Gaskell, Jane. "What Counts as Skill? Reflections on Pay Equity." In *Just Wages: A Feminist Assessment of Pay Equity.* Edited by Judy Fudge and Patricia McDermott. University of Toronto Press, 1991.

Giles, Wenona. *Motherhood and Wage Labour in London: Portuguese Migrant Workers and the Politics of Gender.* Ph.D Thesis, University of Toronto, 1987.

___. "Class, Gender and Race Struggles in a Portuguese Neighbourhood in London." *International Journal of Urban and Regional Research*, 15, 3 (1991): 432-441.

___. "Gender Inequality and Resistance: The Case of Portuguese Women in London." *Anthropological Quarterly*, 65, 2 (1992): 67-79.

___. "Clean Jobs, Dirty Jobs: Ethnicity, Social Reproduction and Gendered Identity." *Culture*, 1994 forthcoming.

Gilman, Charlotte Perkins. *Women and Economics.* New York: Harper and Row, 1966.

___. *The Home: Its Work and Influence.* Chicago: The University of Illinois Press, 1972

Giminez, Martha. "Waged Work, Domestic Labor and Household Survival in the United States." In *Work Without Wages.* Edited by Jane Collins and Martha Giminez. Albany: SUNY Press, 1990, p. 25n.

Glenn, Evelyn Nakano. "Racial Ethnic Women's Labour: The Intersection of Race, Gender and Class Oppression." *Review of Radical Political Economy*, 17, 3 (1985): 86-108.

___. *Issei, Nisei, War Bride: Three Generations of Japanese American Women in Domestic Service.* Philadelphia: Temple University Press, 1986.

___. "From Servitude to Service Work: Historical Continuities in the Racial Division of Paid Labour." *Signs:Journal of Women in Culture and Society*, 18, 1 (1992): 1-43.

REFERENCES

Globe and Mail. "Immigration Review Worries Domestic Workers." January 6, 1990, A5.

Goelman, H., (1992). "Day Care in Canada" in *Child Care in Context: Cross-Cultural Perspectives.* Edited by M.Lamb, K.Sternberg, C.Hwang, and A.Broberg. New Jersey: Lawrence Erlbaum Publishers, 1992.

Gowen, Sara. "Invisible Workers: An International Cleaners Conference." *Spare Rib,* 187 (1988): 20-23.

Griffin, S. *To Professionalize or Unionize: Is that the Question?* Victoria: School of Child Care, University of Victoria, 1989.

Grigg v. Duke Power Co. 401 U.S. 424 (1971).

Hadley, Karen. Ph.D Thesis. Ontario Institute for Studies in Education, forthcoming.

Harms, T., and Clifford, R. *Early Childhood Environment Rating Scale.* Columbia University, New York: Teachers College Press, 1980.

Harris, J. *Portuguese Workers in the United Kingdom.* A study commissioned by the Portuguese Institute of Immigration,The Portuguese Consulate. Unpublished manuscript, London, 1978.

Hartmann, Heidi. "Capitalism, Patriarchy and Job Segregation by Sex." *Signs: Journal of Women in Culture and Society,* 1, 3 (1976): 137-169.

____. "The Unhappy Marriage of Marxism and Feminism: Towards a More Progressive Union." In *Women and Revolution.* Edited by Lydia Sargent. Boston: Pluto Press, 1981.

Hayden, Dolores. *The Grand Domestic Revolution.* Cambridge: MIT Press, 1981.

Hertz, Rosanna. *More Equal Than Others: Women and Men in Dual Career Marriages.* Berkeley: University of California Press, 1986.

Hochschild, Arlie Russell. *The Managed Heart: The Commercialization of Human Feeling.* Berkeley: University of California Press, 1983.

____. *The Second Shift: Working Parents and the Revolution at Home.* New York: Avon Books, 1990.

Hollingsworth, Laura. *The FASWOC Strike, 1984—A Description and An Analysis.* Unpublished paper, Sociology Department, University of Toronto, 1986.

hooks, bell. *Ain't I a woman: Black women and feminism.* Boston: South End Press, 1981.

____. *Feminist Theory:From Margin to Center.* Boston: South End Press, 1984.

Immigration Regulations as amended SOR/78-172, 1978.

INTERCEDE. *Report and Recommendations on the Foreign Domestic Movement Program.* Toronto, 1990.

Jackson, Nancy. "Who Gains from the New Skills Training?" *Women's Education,* 5, 2 (1986):10-13.

Jacoby, Russell. *Social Amnesia.* Boston: Beacon Press, 1975.

James, Selma. *Women, the Unions and Work.* Bristol: Falling Wall Press, 1976.

Jorde Bloom, P. "Professional Orientation: Individual and Organizational Perspectives," *Child and Youth Care Quarterly 18* (Winter 1989).

Kailisch, Beatrice and Philip. *Politics of Nursing.* Philadelphia: J. B. Lippincott, 1982.

Karyo Communications, Inc. *Executive Summary: Caring For a Living.* Ottawa: Canadian Child Day Care Federation and Canadian Day Care Advocacy Association, 1992.

____.*Together: In Pursuit of Quality.* The 22nd annual conference proceedings. Rich-

133

mond, B.C.: Early Childhood Educators of British Columbia, 1992.

Katzman, David. *Seven Days a Week: Women and Domestic Service in Industrializing America*. Chicago: University of Illinois Press, 1981.

Klein, Suzanne Silk. Ontario Ministry of Labour—policy. Telephone Interview with Author. October 16, 1990.

Kleinman, Carol. "Maid Services Clean Up as Demand Escalates." *Chicago Tribune*, August 17, 1986, section 8, p. 1.

Knight, I. "Patterns of Labour Mobility in the Hotel and Catering Industry." *Manpower in the Hotel and Catering Industry*. London: Hotel and Catering Industry Training Board, 1978.

Labelle, M., G. Turcotte, Kempeneers, M., and D. Meintel. *Histoires d'Immigrées, Itineraires d'Ouvriéres Colombiennes, Greques, Haitiennes et Portugaises de Montréal*. Montreal: Boreal, 1987.

Lamphere, Louise. *From Working Daughters to Working Mothers: Immigrant Women in a New England Industrial Community*. Ithaca, N.Y.: Cornell University Press, 1987.

Landes, Joan. "Wages for Housework—Political and Theoretical Considerations." In *The Politics of Housework*. Edited by E. Malos. London: Allison and Busby, 1980.

Legrange, A., and Malcolm Read. *Those Who Care: A report on child caregivers in Alberta day care centres*. Red Deer: Child Care Matters, 1990.

Lenin, V.I. *On the Emancipation of Women*. New York: International Publishers, 1972.

Leslie, Genevieve. "Domestic Service in Canada, 1880-1920." *Women at Work: 1850-1930*. Edited by J. Acton. Toronto: Women's Educational Press, 1980.

Levenstein, Aaron. *Why People Work*. New York: Crowell, 1962.

Livingstone, David and Meg Luxton. "Gender Consciousness at Work: Modifications of the Male Breadwinner Norm Among Steelworkers and Their Spouses." *The Canadian Review of Sociology and Anthropology*, 26, 2 (1989): 240-275.

Luxton, Meg and Heather Jon Maroney. "Begetting Babies; Raising Children: The Politics of Parenting." *The Crisis in Socialist Theory, Strategy and Practice*. Vol. 7, Society for Socialist Studies, 1992.

Lycklama, Geertje. *Trade in Domestic Helpers: Causes, Mechanisms and Consequences*. Selected papers from the planning meeting on international migration and women, Quezon City, Philippines 30 November—5 December 1987. Kuala Lumpur: Asia and Pacific Development Centre, 1989.

MacKenzie, S. "Building Women, Building Cities: Toward Gender Sensitive Theory in the Environmental Disciplines." In *Life Spaces: Gender, Household, Employment*. Edited by C. Andrew and B.M. Milroy. Vancouver: U.B.C. Press, 1988.

MacKinnon, Catherine. *Toward a Feminist Theory of the State*. Cambridge: Harvard University Press, 1983.

Maldonada, Caroline. *Development of a G.L.C. Policy on Migrants and Refugees*. Unpublished report. Principal Race Relations Advisor, Greater London Council, 1983.

Malos, Ellen, ed. *The Politics of Housework*. London: Allison and Busby, 1980.

Martin, Linda and Kerry Segrave. *The Servant Problem: Domestic Workers in North*

America. Jefferson: McFarland and Co. Inc., 1985.

Marx, Karl. *Capital. Volume I.* Harmondsworth, U.K.: New Left Review, Penguin, 1976.

Matthaei, Julie. *An Economic History of Women in America: Women's Work, the Sexual Division of Labour and the Development of Capitalism.* New York: Schocken, 1982.

Mayes, Brian. Report for the Committee for Cleaners' Rights, research June-August, 1987.

McDermott, Patricia. "The Eaton's Strike: We Wouldn't Have Missed It for the World." In *Women Challenging Unions: Feminism, Democracy and Militancy.* Edited by Linda Linda Briskin and Patricia McDermott. Toronto: University of Toronto Press, 1993.

Medlik, S. *Profile of the Hotel and Catering Industry.* London: Heinemann, 1978.

Meintel, D., M. Labelle, G. Turcotte, and M. Kempeneers. "Migration, Wage Labour and Domestic Relationships: Immigrant Women Workers in Montreal." *Anthropologica,* 26, 2 (1985): 135-169.

___. "The New Double Workday of Immigrant Women Workers in Quebec." *Women's Studies,* 13, 3 (1987): 273-293.

Mies, Maria, V. Bennholdt-Thomsen, and C. Von Werlhof. *Women: The Last Colony.* London: Zed Books, 1988.

Morokvasic, Mirjana. "Fortress Europe and Migrant Women." *Feminist Review,* 39 (1991): 69-84.

Murphy, Rosemary. "Nurse as/and Mother." In *Limited Edition: Voices of Women, Voices of Feminism.* Edited by Geraldine Finn. Halifax: Fernwood Publishing: 1993.

Myles, John, Garnett Picot, and Ted Wannell. *Wages and Jobs in the Eighties: Changing Youth Wages and the Declining Middle.* Research Paper No. 17. Ottawa: Statistics Canada, 1988.

Nash, June and Patricia Fernandez-Kelly. *Women, Men and the International Division of Labour.* Albany N.Y.: SUNY Press, 1983.

National Action Committee on the Status of Women. *Review of the Situation of Canadian Women.* Toronto, 1991.

National Association for the Education of the Young Child. *Investing in Quality.* Washington, D.C., 1990.

Nations Restaurant News. June 6, 1988.

Neal, Rusty. *Cleaning Up in Public: Women's Experiences as Subcontracted Cleaners.* M.A. Thesis, Ontario Institute for Studies in Education, 1988.

Nicholson, Linda. *Gender and History: The Limits of Social Theory in the Age of the Family.* New York: Columbia University Press, 1986.

Ng, Roxana and Alma Estable. "Immigrant Women in the Labour Force: An Overview of Present Knowledge and Research Gaps." *Resources for Feminist Research,* 16, 1 (1987): 29.

Norpark Computer, Inc. *Description of Child Care Training Programs in Canadian and International Jurisdictions.* Toronto: Child Care Branch, Ministry of Community and Social Services (October, 1991).

___. *Training Needs of Resource Teachers, Supervisors of Day Nurseries and Private Home Day Care Visitors.* Toronto: Child Care Branch, Ministry of Community and

Social Services (October, 1991).

Ontario, Government of. *Labour Relations Act R.S.O.* 1980, as amended in 1986, chapter 228.

___. *Report of July-September 1984*, Labour Relations Board, p. 931-937.

___. *Employment Standards Act*, 1986.

Osberg, L. *The Economics of National Standards*. Toronto: Government of Ontario, 1992.

Palmer Phyllis. *Domesticity and Dirt: Housewives and Domestic Servants in the United States, 1920-1945.* Philadelphia: Temple University Press, 1989.

Parr, Joy. *The Gender of Breadwinners Women, Men and Change in Two Industrial Towns, 1880-1950.* University of Toronto Press, 1990.

Paul, Jane. *Where There's Muck There's Money: A Report on the Cleaning Industry in London.* Greater London Council, 1984.

Pearson, Philip. *Twilight Robbery: Trade Unions and Low Paid Workers in Britain Today.* London: Pluto Press, 1985.

Pereira de Melo, Hildete. "Feminists and Domestic Workers in Rio de Janeiro." In *Muchachas No More.* Edited by Elsa Chaney and Mary Garcia Castro. Philadelphia: Temple University Press, 1989, p. 245n.

Pessar, Patricia. "The Linkage Between the Household and Workplace of Dominican Women in the U.S." *International Migration Review,* 18 (1984): 1188-1211.

Petrykanyn, John. "Foreign Domestic Workers and Misrepresentations: New Policy, Old Practices?" *Immigration & Citizenship Bulletin,* 1, 8 (November/December 1989): 3n.

Phillips. A. and B. Taylor. "Sex and Skill: Notes Toward a Feminist Economics." *Feminist Review,* 6(1980): 79-78.

Portes, A. "The Informal Sector: Definition, Controversy and Relation to National Development." *Review,* 8, 1 (1983): 151-174.

Powell, D., and A. Stremmel. "The relation of early childhood training and experience to the professional development of child care workers." *Early Childhood Research Quarterly 4* (1989).

Pragnell, Bradley J. *Organizing Department Store Workers: The Case of RWDSU at Eaton's 1983-1987.* Industrial Relations Centre, Queen's University, Research Report # 22, 1989.

Ramsay, E. "Caught in the Housing Trap: Employees in Tied Housing." *CES Research Series No. 31 and Survey of Hotel and Catering Vacancies Advertised in Job Centres.* Unpublished manuscript, 1978.

Redclift, N. and E. Mingione. *Beyond Employment: Household, Gender and Subsistence.* Oxford: Basil Blackwell, 1985.

Reiter, Ester. *Making Fast Food: From the Frying Pan into the Fryer.* Montreal and Kingston: McGill-Queen's University Press, 1991.

Roberts, Barbara. "'A Work of Empire': Canadian Reformers and British Female Immigration." In *A Not Unreasonable Claim: Women and Reform in Canada 1880s-1920s.* Edited by L. Kealey. Toronto: The Women's Press, 1979.

Robertson, David, James Rinehart, Christopher Huxley, and the CAW Research Group on CAMI. "Team Concept and *Kaizen*: Japanese Production Management in a Unionized Canadian Auto Plant." *Studies in Political Economy*, 39 (Autumn 1992): 77-107.

Rollins, Judith. *Between Women: Domestics and Their Employers*. Philadelphia: Temple University Press, 1985.

Romero, Mary. *Maid in the U.S.A.* New York: Routledge, 1992.

Rosenberg, Harriet. "The Home is the Workplace: Hazards, Stress and Pollutants in the Household." In *Through the Kitchen Window: The Politics of Home and Family*. Edited by M. Luxton, H. Rosenberg, and S. Arat-Koc. Toronto: Garamond Press, 1990.

Ross, Joanne and John Calvert. "Slice by Slice: Contracting Out at the Toronto School Board." *OurSchools/Ourselves*, 1, 1 (1988): 106-118.

Runneymede Trust. "Migrant Workers in Britain. Background Paper." *Runneymede Trust Bulletin*, 164 (February 1984).

Rustin, Michael. "The Politics of Post-Fordism: Or, The Trouble with 'New Times.'" *New Left Review*, 175 (May/June 1989).

Sacks, Karen. *Caring by the Hour: Women, Work and Organizing at Duke University Medical Center*. Urbana: University of Illinois Press, 1988.

Sanjek, Roger. "Maid Servants and Market Women's Apprentices in Adabraka." In *At Work in Homes: Household Workers in World Perspective*. Edited by R. Sanjek and S. Colen. Washington: American Ethnological Society, 1990.

Sanjek, Roger and Shellee Colen, eds. *At Work in Homes: Household Workers in World Perspective*. Washington: American Ethnological Society, 1990.

Sassen-Koob, Saskia. "Notes on the Incorporation of Third World Women into Wage Labour Through Immigration and Off-Shore Production." *International Migration Review*, 18, 4 (1984): 144-167.

___. "Changing Composition and Labour Market Location of Hispanic Immigrants in New York City, 1960-1980." In *Hispanics in the U.S. Economy*. Edited by G. Borjas and M. Tienda. New York: Academic Press, 1985.

Seager, Joni and Ann Olson. *Women in the World: An International Atlas*. London: Pan Books, 1986.

Schom-Moffat, P. "The bottom line: Wages and working conditions for workers in the formal day care market." A report prepared for the *Task Force on Child Care, Series 1*. Ottawa: Status of Women Canada, 1990.

Seccombe, Wally. "Reflections on the Domestic Labour Debate and Prospects for Marxist-feminist Synthesis." In *The Politics of Diversity: Feminism, Marxism and Nationalism*. Edited by Roberta Hamilton and Michele Barrett. London: Verso, 1986.

Seto-Thomas, L. *Native Child Care*. Ottawa: Native Council of Canada, 1990.

Silvera, Makeda. *Silenced*. Toronto: Williams-Wallace Publishers, 1983.

___. *Silenced*. Second Edition. Toronto: Sister Vision, 1989.

Sinclair, Jim. *Crossing the Line*. Vancouver: New Star Press, 1992.

Skinner, Joseph F. "Big Mac and the Tropical Forests." *Monthly Review*, 37, 7 (December 1985):25-32.

Sklair, Leslie. *Sociology of the Global System*. Baltimore: Johns Hopkins Press, 1991.

Slaughter, Jane and Mike Parker. *Choosing Sides*. Boston: South End Press, 1991.

Smith, Vivian. "Rules Yield to Need for Nannies." *Globe and Mail*, March 4, 1994: A1, A5).

Spelman, Elizabeth. *The Inessential Woman: Problems of Exclusion in Feminist Thought*. Boston: Beacon Press.

Stainsby, Mia. "Powerless: The Plight Faction Foreign Domestic Workers in B.C." *Vancouver Sun*, November 10, 1989.

Stasiulis, Daiva. "Rainbow Feminism: Perspectives on Minority Women in Canada." *Resources for Feminist Research*, 16, 1 (1987): 5.

Strauss, Marina. "First You Have to Get the Attention of Teens." *Globe and Mail Report on Business*, July 12, 1991, p. B1.

Taylor, Barbara. *Eve and the New Jerusalem: Socialism and Feminism in the Nineteenth Century*. London: Virago Press, 1983.

Tilly, Louise. "Paths of Proletarianization: Organization of Production, Sexual Division of Labour, and Women's Collective Action." *Signs*, 7, 21 (1981).

Tucker, Susan. *Telling Memories Among Southern Women: Domestic Workers and Their Employers in the Segregated South*. Baton Rouge: Louisiana State University Press, 1988.

Turritin, Jane. "Doing Domestic: Work Relationships in a Particularistic Setting." In *Work in the Canadian Context*. Edited by K. Lundy and B. Warme. Toronto: Butterworths, 1981, p. 93n.

United Kingdom, Department of Employment. "Work Permits by Country of Origin and Industrial Group." *Gazette*, 1925–1980. London, U.K.

Walzer, Michael. *Spheres of Justice*. New York: Basic Books, 1983.

Ward, Kathryn. *Women Workers and Global Restructuring*. Ithaca. N.Y.: ILR Press, Cornell University, 1990.

Waring, Marilyn. *If Women Counted: The New Feminist Economics*. San Francisco: Harper and Row, 1988.

Weinbaum, Batya and Amy Bridges. "The Other Side of the Paycheck: Monopoly Capital and the Structure of Capitalism." In *Capitalist Patriarchy and the Case for Socialist Feminism*. Edited by Z. Eisenstein. New York: Monthly Review Press, 1979.

West Coast Domestic Workers Association. *Summary of Results: Foreign Domestic Worker Employment Survey*. Vancouver, March 1990.

Wheeler, Karen. *Interim Report to the Committee for Cleaners Rights*, January 28, 1987, p. 2.

Whitebook, M., Howes, C., and D. Philips *Who cares? Child care teachers and the quality of care in America*. Final report of the Child Care Staffing Study, Oakland, California, (1990).

Yuval-Davis, Nira. "The Citizenship Debate: Women, Ethnic Processes and the State." *Feminist Review*, 39 (1991).

Yuval-Davis, Nira and Floya Anthias, eds. *Woman-Nation-State*. London: MacMillan Press, 1989.